MW01234386

The Fall of a Godly Nation

By Jim Davenport

ISBN 978-1-312-56076-5

Lulu Paperback Edition

For information please address:
Jim Davenport
InfoSys Solutions Associates, Inc.
6637 Burnt Hickory Drive
Hoschton, GA 30548

http://jimdavenport.me/
jamesldavenport@gmail.com

Jim's books are also available in eBook and Hardback Editions
Preview and Order Books by Jim Davenport
http://jimdavenport.me/jims-books/

Book Description

The Bible teaches that the fall of Israel and Judah as once Godly nations resulted from their own continued sinfulness and disobedience to God's commands ... not from the strength and power of their enemies. In this book the author focuses on a portion of the history of Israel and Judah stretching from 750 BC to 586 BC and in particular the leadership of King Hezekiah and his son Manasseh. Parallels are drawn between the sinfulness of Israel/Judah and modern-day America.

Topics covered include the positive reforms of Hezekiah such as the revival of the worship of Yahweh; the building of Hezekiah's Tunnel; the lies, intimidation and blasphemy of Assyria's King Sennacherib; Hezekiah's illness unto death and his miraculous recovery; the consequences of Hezekiah's pride; and the failure of Hezekiah as a Godly father in rearing his son Manasseh. The final chapter deals with what will be required for God to Save America from a similar downfall.

Note: All scripture quoted or referenced in this book is from the English Standard Version (ESV) of the Bible unless otherwise noted. ESV - Copyright 2001 by Crossway Bibles, a ministry of the Good News Publishers of Wheaton, Illinois, U.S.

Contents

... **Dedication**

This book is dedicated to my beloved wife and best friend Charlotte, who next to the Lord Jesus means more to me than anyone or anything else in this whole world!

Charlotte is patient, kind and loving no matter the situation. She allows me plenty of space to concentrate on my writing without even a hint of complaint. I know there are times that I neglect both her and my role as her husband, yet she never complains.

Charlotte patiently reads all of my manuscripts and provides insightful and honest feedback. Without her I couldn't do much of anything. I love Charlotte with all of my heart and thank God every day for putting us together for life more than fifty years ago. Thank you God for the wonderful gift of Charlotte!

I also dedicate this book to our faithful son and daughter in law, Keven and Amy Davenport; our granddaughter Ashlyn, her husband Josh Murphy, and their two children Sawyer and Rhory; and to our grandson Mason Davenport ... each of whom I love with all my heart and thank God for each day!

... About Jim Davenport

Jim Davenport resides in the USA in Northeast Georgia, is a member of a Southern Baptist Church and is a retired Christian business man. Jim and his wife Charlotte have one son and daughter in law, Keven and Amy, three grandchildren – Ashlyn (Davenport) and husband Josh Murphy, and Mason Davenport. We have two great-grandchildren, Sawyer Joshua Murphy (May 9, 2013 – May 27, 2013) and Rhory Camille Murphy (born September 4, 2014.)

Jim and Charlotte own a mountain get-away home located on Lookout Mountain in Alabama where they spend many spring, summer and fall days working in their raised bed organic garden. Jim has served as a Deacon and Trustee in his local church most of his adult life and on the Executive Committee and Finance Committee of the Board of Trustees of Shorter University, an intentionally Christian institution located in Rome, Georgia.

Jim has a passion for the word of God and has always believed that Christian principles should guide every aspect of his life. He also loves Christian music and often served as a tenor soloist in his church. One of the highlights of his life was the nearly 20 years he spent singing with The Good News, a Southern Gospel quartet.

Jim served as an Information Technology professional his entire working career of 50 years holding senior positions in and consulting with hundreds of world-class organizations in the United States, Canada, Europe, Central and South America, Australia and New Zealand.

Jim remains as President and CEO of InfoSys Solutions Associates, Inc. and is a retired partner of IT Governance

Partners, LLC, both of which are "Trusted Advisor" technology and business consulting firms.

Jim has authored three books and is in the process of finishing a fourth. His blog is regularly read by readers from more than 120 countries.

Jim holds both a BS and an MS in Mathematics from Georgia State University in Atlanta, Georgia and completed Management Development Training at Emory University in Atlanta, Georgia.

... About My Blog
http://jimdavenport.me/

I am not an accomplished author by any stretch of the imagination. But I do enjoy writing about subjects that are important to me. I have spent much of my life in the information technology and consulting fields overseeing the successful preparation and presentation of tens of thousands of pages of complex technical and business documentation. At the same time, I have not written that much about what is really important to me ... namely, sharing my Christian life experience with others in hopes that it would be meaningful to them in their Christian walk. Over the years as a Sunday School teacher at Pine Lake Baptist Church in Stone Mountain, Georgia, I put together hundreds of notes and outlines to guide my teaching. I always intended to develop some of those notes into a series of articles.

In late 2010 as my business career began to wind down and after suffering some health issues, I realized that I needed to move on with the development of the articles post haste. So I started a "blog" site using Wordpress.com to post articles as each was completed.

At times my posts are rather passionate and touch on subjects that are controversial. Admittedly, my posts are not very scholarly and are often quite opinionated. However, I always try to provide ample scripture to back up my points.

I realize that not everyone will appreciate my point of view, but my prayer is that I will make you think ... and in particular think about your relationship to our Lord and Savior, Jesus Christ. Your courteous comments are always welcome.

Please visit my blog site, **http://jimdavenport.me/**, for additional articles and information about Jim Davenport.

Foreword

I was born during World War II in the deep south of the United States of America ... what was (and to some degree still is) commonly known as "The Bible Belt." There were churches in every town and community and on just about every major intersection close to where I lived. And just about everyone that we knew attended church. We were surrounded by Christian family and friends.

After World War II ended America witnessed a building boom like none ever experienced before. Neighborhoods grew up in the suburbs of the south's major cities and each seemed anchored by community churches. Business was conducted on Monday through Saturday and Sunday was devoted to worship. Neighbors looked after neighbors. Children played safely in their neighborhoods near their homes. They engaged in games like "hide and seek" and "kick the can." They caught June bugs in the day and lightning bugs after dark. They rode bicycles endlessly. Families attended spring and fall revivals at their churches. They worshiped together, prayed together, had dinner on the grounds together, had regular ice-cream socials together. Times seemed safer then ... totally absent of today's ever-present threat of terrorism in our homeland.

I have lived through some grand times and some tumultuous times in America. But I must now say that nothing I have previously experienced matches what our nation faces today. Once we were thought of as a **Godly Nation** ... a nation of laws founded on Judeo/Christian principles ... a nation free to practice religion without government mandate or government intervention.

But things have drastically changed over the years. As a nation, we have turned away from those basic Judeo/Christian principles. America is on the verge of a total moral collapse. Our citizens are divided. To an ever growing number it is offensive to refer to America as a "Godly Nation."

I believe we are witnessing the repeat of what happened to Israel/Judah more than 2,500-2,750 years ago. Just as in the times of Isaiah, "All we like sheep have gone astray; we have turned—every one—to his own way; and the LORD has laid on Him the iniquity of us all (Isaiah 53:6 ESV).

Is America going to repeat history and go the way of Israel/Judah? History is our teacher. God has been patient with America ... a once **Godly Nation**. Israel/Judah was also a once **Godly Nation**. Israel/Judah suffered their fall. Will America be next to experience **"The Fall of a Godly Nation?"** Only time will tell.

Jim Davenport

September, 2014

01 – An Introduction to a Series of Articles on Ancient Israel and Judah That Parallel Our Modern Day

Background:

The Twelve Tribes of Israel

For quite some time I have been reading and studying chronologically the section of Scripture that deals with the time period 750 BC to 586 BC. Israel's glory years led by David and his son Solomon had long ended and were followed by two monarchies split into northern and southern kingdoms after the northern tribes would not accept Solomon's son and David's grandson, Rehoboam, as their king. Instead the northern tribes brought back Jereboam from Egypt as their king and hostilities existed between the two kingdoms for an extended period of time.

Gradually each of the kingdoms eroded, falling further away from God and into idolatry. There were periods where hope sprung forth, only to be quenched again and again by a return to sinful degeneration. A number of prophets warned of the impending punishment because of Israel's failure to keep their covenant with Yahweh.

—

The Two Monarchy Kingdoms of Israel and Judah

Throughout the period Israel and Judah basically served as vassal states first to the Neo-Assyrian Empire, then to the Neo-Babylonian Empire. Ultimately both kingdoms fell to their enemies and most of the survivors were swept away into captivity and pseudo-slavery reminiscent of their time in Egypt.

Portions of a number of Old Testament Scriptures record the events for the time period including 2 Kings, 2 Chronicles, Isaiah, Zephaniah, Amos, Jonah, Micah, Jeremiah, Proverbs, Hosea, Nahum, Habakkuk, Daniel, Ezekiel, Lamentations, Obadiah and Psalms.

The northern kingdom of Israel was under constant attack from Assyria for decades. With the sacking of Samaria (the capital city of Israel) in 722 BC, all ten tribes of the northern kingdom fell to the Neo-Assyrian Empire. The long and bloody warfare leading to their fall was conducted in multiple waves by the Assyrian monarchs Tiglath-Pileser III (747-727 BC), Shalmaneser V (727-722 BC), and Sargon II (722-705 BC). The Bible records that Israel's defeat was because "... *the children of **Israel had sinned** against the Lord their God ...* (see 2 Kings 17:5-12)."

Meanwhile, the Southern Kingdom of Judah, consisting of the two tribes of Judah and Benjamin, was still standing, though weakly. The Assyrians attempted to take the city of Jerusalem during their Northern campaigns in Israel; however, God did **not yet** allow that to happen. BUT, Judah would not escape God's punishment ... and for much the same reason as that of Israel. In 2 Kings 17:13-14 the Bible records "*Yet the Lord testified against Israel **and against Judah**, by ALL of His prophets, every seer, saying, "**Turn from your evil ways**, and **keep My commandments** and My statutes, according to all the law which I commanded your fathers, and which I sent to you by My servants the prophets." **Nevertheless they would not hear**, but **stiffened their necks**, like the necks of their fathers, who did not believe in the Lord their God.*"

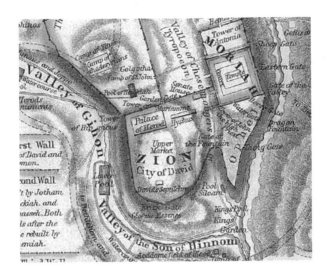

Jerusalem and The Valley of Hinnon

Judah, just like Israel, adopted and tolerated the worship of pagan gods from their surrounding neighbors. Unholy alliances with foreign governments and politically motivated marriages were common in that day in an attempt to protect their home land from foreign invasion. The kings of Judah even allowed idols of other gods to be placed in the Temple to be worshiped side by side with Yahweh, the true and only God.

Molech Worship – Valley of Hinnon

Sanctuaries were built in what the Scripture calls "high places" dating back to Solomon's time. These "high places" were worship and sacrifice centers for pagan gods. Even child sacrifices to the pagan god Molech took place (see my article "On Child Sacrifice") at Tophet, the cultic site in the Valley of Hinnon (2 Kings 23:10) on the south side of Jerusalem ultimately known as Gehenna (hell fire) in New Testament times.

Because of both their individual and collective sin, Judah ultimately fell to the Neo-Babylonian Empire. Four deportations of Judah's Jews took place between 605 BC and 582 BC and the captivity lasted for 70 years before they began returning to their homeland after the fall of Babylon to the Persians under King Cyrus.

Scripture: (all NKJV unless otherwise noted)

Micah 6:8 – *He has **shown** you, O man, **what is good**; And what does the Lord require of you But to **do justly**, To **love mercy**, And to **walk humbly** with your God?*

Isaiah 29:14-16 – *[14] Therefore, behold, I will again do a marvelous work Among this people, A marvelous work and a wonder; For the **wisdom of their wise men shall perish**, And the **understanding of their prudent men shall be hidden**."[15] Woe to those who seek deep to **hide their counsel** far from the Lord, And their works are in the dark; They say, "**Who sees us?**" and, "**Who knows us?**" [16] **Surely you have things turned around!** Shall the potter be esteemed as the clay; For shall the thing made say of him who made it, "**He did not make me**"? Or shall the thing formed say of him who formed it, "He has no understanding"?*

Discussion:

The problems for Israel and Judah dated back to the time when they entered the Promised Land. God gave them that land, told them to occupy it and to purge it of ALL of its present inhabitants. However, thinking they knew more than God, they left many of the pagans alive. Over time their sin compounded as they intermarried with the foreigners often adopting the worship of their gods alongside of Yahweh.

God had clearly shown them "*... **what is good**" and "... **what the Lord require(d) of them** ...* (Micah 6:8)." But they thought that they could "cheat" God by applying their own definition of what is good and what God required of them. They continued in their sin compounding their situation further, all the time thinking that their ways and solutions were better than those of God. Sounds familiar doesn't it!

The prophet Isaiah spoke to them repeatedly, as did others, about their folly and the application of their own wisdom over God's wisdom. Through Isaiah God told them "... *their wise men shall perish, and the understanding of their prudent men shall be hidden*" (Isaiah 29:14). The foolishness of their ways in thinking that they knew more than God is clearly seen in God's further statement in verses 15-16: "*15 Woe to those who seek deep to **hide their counsel far from the Lord**, And their works are in the dark; They say, "Who sees us?" and, "Who knows us?" 16 Surely you have things turned around!* Shall the potter be esteemed as the clay; For shall the thing made say of him who made it, "**He did not make me**"? Or shall the thing formed say of him who formed it, "He has no understanding"?*

The gradual erosion and sinful decay of Israel and Judah ultimately led to their complete downfall including the devastation of their precious Promised Land, captivity in an unfamiliar foreign country, and forced slavery to their captors.

Reflection:

I see such a strong parallel between Israel and Judah to our modern-day world. In particular, the United States of America ... so blessed by God over our history ... has turned almost totally away from God's teachings. Only a remnant remains faithful and lives in accordance with God's commands. Our government and our national news media even discriminate against Christians while at the same time demanding and protecting the rights of other religions such as Islam. From all appearances, the USA is over the line with God as a nation. God must look at us in ALL of His righteousness and weep. We depend on our "wise men" that are out of touch with Almighty God, constantly bickering with each other, hardly ever agreeing on anything, substituting their own wisdom over that of God. In God's righteousness He will not continue to overlook our individual and collective sin. There are consequences that must and will be paid here on earth and eternally.

02 – Hezekiah Brings Reforms and Revival to Judah

Background:

Hezekiah – A Righteous King of Judah

King Hezekiah was a descendant of the House of David and reigned over Judah for 29 years from 716 to 687 BC[1] His father was King Ahaz. Hezekiah served as co-regent with his father from 729 BC to 716 BC. He became co-regent when he was twelve years old. When Ahaz died in 716 BC Hezekiah assumed his role as king. Hezekiah's son, Manasseh, served as co-regent alongside his father beginning in 700 BC at the age of 12, just as his father had done. Hezekiah died when he was

54 years old and Manasseh became sole king of Judah in 687 BC. A future article in this series will deal with Manasseh.

The Bible records that King Hezekiah faithfully served Yahweh. He is favorably remembered in Jewish and Christian history as a "good king" (2 Chronicles 29:1).

King Sennacherib of Assyria in Royal Dress – This painted sketch is of the mighty Assyrian king Sennacherib relief which was discovered on the walls of his palace in Khorsabad, near the ruins of ancient Nineveh.

Hezekiah ascended to the throne in a very troubled time for Judah. His "rotten"[2] father, Ahaz, had not been a good king. Ahaz promoted pagan worship destroying the godly work of his father, King Jotham, and his grandfather, King Uzziah.

The Assyrian Empire under Sargon II had conquered the northern kingdom of Israel and carried off the ten northern tribes into captivity. Under King Ahaz Judah had agreed to pay an annual tribute to Assyria to maintain their independence and safety as a vassal state. However, this arrangement only placated the Assyrians until Sargon II died and was succeeded by his son Sennacherib in 705 BC.

Initially Hezekiah withheld the tribute from Sennacherib thinking that he might have an opening with this new ruler. Sennacherib responded by sending a letter to Hezekiah telling him that he was mounting an attack on Jerusalem and that he should surrender because the gods of Assyria were stronger than Yahweh. Unfortunately for Sennacherib his plan completely backfired when "The Angel of the Lord" (Yahweh, the only true God), brought about the death of Sennacherib's entire invading army of 185,000 in one night (2 Kings 19:35-37) without any help from Judah. The Bible records that with this "… *Sennacherib king of Assyria departed and went away, returned home, and remained at Nineveh …*" and as he was worshiping his pagan god "*his sons Adrammelech and Sharezer struck him down with the sword; and they escaped into the land of Ararat. Then Esarhaddon his son reigned in his place.*"

Scripture: (all NKJV unless otherwise noted)

2 Chronicles 30:21-27 – *²¹ So the children of Israel who were present at Jerusalem kept the Feast of Unleavened Bread seven days with great gladness; and the Levites and the priests praised the Lord day by day, singing to the Lord, accompanied by loud instruments. ²² And **Hezekiah gave encouragement to all the Levites who taught the good knowledge of the Lord**; and they ate throughout the feast seven days, offering peace offerings and making confession to the Lord God of their fathers. ²³ Then the whole assembly agreed to **keep the feast another seven days**, and they kept it another seven days with*

*gladness. [24] For Hezekiah king of Judah gave to the assembly a thousand bulls and seven thousand sheep, and the leaders gave to the assembly a thousand bulls and ten thousand sheep; and a great number of priests sanctified themselves. [25] The **whole assembly of Judah rejoiced**, also the priests and Levites, all the assembly that came from Israel, the sojourners who came from the land of Israel, and those who dwelt in Judah. [26] **So there was great joy in Jerusalem, for since the time of Solomon the son of David, king of Israel, there had been nothing like this in Jerusalem.** [27] Then the priests, the Levites, arose and blessed the people, and their voice was heard; and their prayer came up to His holy dwelling place, to heaven.*

Discussion:

When Hezekiah took over the throne, Judah ... to put it mildly ... was in deep trouble. Their sister kingdom of Israel had fallen to the Assyrians and was seriously threatening to take Judah as well. But early in his reign, Hezekiah took the opposite approach from his father Ahaz and instead followed the way of his grandfather, <u>King Jotham</u>. As a result, Hezekiah returned Judah to the sole and true worship of Yahweh. The anonymous writer of 2 Chronicles records Hezekiah's religious actions in chapters 29-30 that set *"the service of the house of the Lord ... in order* (2 Chronicles 29:35)." The Scripture tells us that Hezekiah:

- restored the Levite priests to all of their temple duties
- repaired and reopened the Jerusalem temple closed by Ahaz
- removed pagan idols and vessels from the temple
- cleansed and sanctified the Jerusalem temple
- centralized the worship of God at the Jerusalem temple
- returned biblical forms of temple sacrifice

- destroyed the "high places" of worship to the foreign gods established by his father
- restored the Passover pilgrimage and celebration (2 Chronicles 30:26)
- required a tithe of the crops
- personally went to the temple and prayed[3]

2 Chronicles 30:21-27 documents in great detail the joyful time in the Jerusalem temple as worshipers participated in the Hezekiah led restoration of the Passover pilgrimage and feast. Hezekiah was so pleased with the celebration that he "... *gave encouragement to all the Levites who taught the good knowledge of the Lord; and they ate throughout the feast seven days, offering peace offerings and making confession to the Lord God of their fathers (2 Chronicles 30:22).* The festivities were so enjoyed that they extended the celebration another seven days (2 Chronicles 30:23). *"So there was great joy in Jerusalem, for since the time of Solomon the son of David, king of Israel, there had been nothing like this in Jerusalem* (2 Chronicles 30:26)."

Praise God ... WHAT A REVIVAL!!

Hezekiah also strengthened Judah politically as he:

- expanded Judah's borders
- entered into a league with Egypt to improve protection (Isaiah 30-31) if attacked[4]
- successfully constructed an underground tunnel to the Gihon Spring outside the walls of Jerusalem to provide water at a new pool (later called the Pool of Siloam) inside the walls of Jerusalem in the event that Jerusalem was under siege and the gates closed

- constructed a <u>broad wall</u> to further protect Jerusalem from Sennacherib's pending attack (Nehemiah 3:8, Isaiah 22:9-10)

Reflection:

The Northern Kingdom of Israel fell to the Assyrians because of their continued disobedience to God. When Hezekiah became King, Judah was still standing and with Hezekiah's **Reforms and Revival** that were ushered in under his leadership, Judah was spared, albeit temporarily. The revival that Hezekiah started was quickly squashed by his son Manasseh when he became King upon Hezekiah's death.

History has much to teach us. You can draw some parallels between the demise of Israel and Judah and the coming demise of the United States of America. The U.S. is most certainly not the favored nation of God's people who were given the Promised Land. But the U.S. has definitely been the beneficiary of God's favor and His grace over our 239 year history as an independent nation. There have been times of war, depression, drought, disasters, internal strife and a myriad of other difficult obstacles to overcome. But our country still stands … at least politically speaking … though many are forecasting the end of our nation as we have known it. I have lived through 70 of the 239 years of our existence and I submit that I have never been more disappointed in my country than I am now. Our leadership is corrupt. The majority of our people have abandoned their religion, their faith and the local church. Our focus as a people on Almighty God and abiding by His commands and statutes has eroded to the point that it is out of vogue and even derisive to be called a Christian. Christians are attacked by a vocal minority backed by our self-serving national news media.

As Christians it is time for us to stand up for our God and our nation by turning our hearts and lives over to God. It is time for us to live by the Book ... the Bible, God's infallible Word! It is time to allow Jesus to dwell within us and let Him live outward through us. It is time to take man off of the throne and put God back on the throne of our hearts. It is time to support our local church with our attendance and our tithe. It is time to support and work for Godly candidates for political office. It is time for us work against and to vote out leadership that favors the murder of our children, same-sex marriage, undeserved/unwarranted transfer payments, socialistic control of our lives.

As was the case with Hezekiah, one man did make a difference! Through his staunch stand for God a whole nation turned around. BUT, a word of caution here. One man, his son Manasseh, again turned a nation away from God.

To summarize, here are some lessons I derive from this discussion:

- Our work as Christians is never done.
- We are to allow Jesus to live in us and work through us.
- Never give up on God. One person can make a difference.
- Godly Revival leads to cleansing, celebration.

- Revival will not continue if Christians try to do God's work for Him.
- Revival is contagious.
- The Word of God, the Bible, is the ONLY guide and the ONLY definition of all that is good, perfect and right.
- Leadership left unto man and not fostered by God will fail.
- God will use our enemies to bring us down.
- We can often be our own worst enemy.
- There are earthly and eternal consequences to our individual and collective sin.

Where to Read More:

- Scriptures About Hezekiah - 2 Kings 18 - 20; 2 Chronicles 29 - 32; Isaiah 36 - 39
- Biography of King Hezekiah

03 – Successful Execution of the Wrong Plan – Hezekiah's Tunnel

Background:

Revisiting a portion of the second article in this series, <u>Revival Before the Fall</u>, King Hezekiah was a descendant of the <u>House of David</u> and reigned over Judah for 29 years from 716 to 687 BC. His father, King Ahaz, had formed a protective alliance with the Assyrians and even brought the worship of their gods into the Temple (see His reign is described in <u>2 Kings 16</u>; <u>Isaiah 7-9</u>; and <u>2 Chronicles 28</u> for details). Hezekiah served as co-regent with his father from 729 BC to 716 BC beginning at the age of twelve. When Ahaz died in 716 BC Hezekiah assumed his role as king and spent much of his reign reversing what his father put into place.

Cutaway showing how Hezekiah's Tunnel brought fresh water from the Gihon Spring inside the walls of Jerusalem, the City of David.

Hezekiah, unlike his father, served Yahweh faithfully and led Judah to a number of religious reforms that set *"**the service of the house of the Lord … in order**"* (2 Chronicles 29:35).

Politically speaking Hezekiah expanded Judah's borders, formed an alliance with Egypt, built a **Broad Wall** to further protect Jerusalem, and successfully constructed an **underground water tunnel** to the Gihon Spring outside the walls of Jerusalem to provide water at a new pool (later called the Pool of Siloam where in John 9 Jesus sent "a man blind from birth" in order to complete his healing) inside the walls of Jerusalem in the event that Jerusalem was under siege and the gates closed. The tunnel was a marvelous engineering achievement, prepared with the knowledge that the Assyrians would eventually attack Jerusalem. It is this latter accomplishment, **Hezekiah's Tunnel**, which is the inspiration for this article.

Scripture: (all ESV unless otherwise noted)

2 Kings 20:20 (NIV) – *As for the other events of Hezekiah's reign, all his achievements and how **he made the pool and the tunnel by which he brought water into the city**, are they not written in the book of the annals of the kings of Judah?*

2 Chronicles 32:2-4 – *²And when Hezekiah saw that Sennacherib had come and intended to fight against Jerusalem, ³he **planned with his officers and his mighty men to stop the water of the springs that were outside the city; and they helped him.** ⁴A great many people were gathered, and they stopped all the springs and the brook that flowed through the land, saying, "Why should the kings of Assyria come and find much water?"*

2 Chronicles 32:30 – *This same **Hezekiah closed the upper outlet of the waters of Gihon and directed them down to the west side of the city of David.** And Hezekiah prospered in all his works.*

Isaiah 22:8-11 - *⁸ He has taken away the covering of Judah. In that day you looked to the weapons of the House of the Forest, ⁹ and you saw that the breaches of the city of David were many.* **You collected the waters of the lower pool,** *¹⁰ and you counted the houses of Jerusalem, and you* **broke down the houses to fortify the wall.** *¹¹ You made a reservoir between the two walls for the water of the old pool.* **But you did not look to Him who did it, or see Him who planned it long ago.**

Discussion:

A bit of history will bring the intended lesson that we will draw from this article into better focus. The Chronological Study Bible published by Thomas Nelson provides the following historical explanation:

> "Beginning in the 8th century B.C. the kingdoms of Judah and Israel were continuously threatened by the Neo-Assyrian Empire. Assyrian kings came to Canaan to collect taxes and to intimidate the local rulers. In 722 B.C. Samaria, the capital of Israel was destroyed (2 Kings 17:6), and those Israelites that could, fled toward Jerusalem. Upon becoming king of Judah in 715 BC Hezekiah did his best to prepare Jerusalem for the eventual attack by the Assyrians. His most lasting project involved water.
>
> Rain in Judah usually comes only in the winter. Thus, Judahites built their cities near perennial springs, and in Jerusalem the main water source was the Gihon spring (1 Kings 1:33, 38). Like most springs, the Gihon flowed in the valley, while the city sat on the hill above. Thus the spring that served Jerusalem water was then, at the foot of the hill outside the walls of the city.

That location would be a problem if an enemy army surrounded the city.

Hezekiah camouflaged the spring and ordered that a tunnel be carved into the hillside to bring water under the city. Shafts were then dug down to the flowing water in the tunnel, which when finished was 1,750 feet long and emptied into the Pool of Siloam (2 Chronicles 32:2-4, 30).

A dedication inscription was discovered in A.D. 1880 near the southern exit of the tunnel. Called the Siloam inscription, it describes the 8-month effort of two teams of diggers working toward each other from opposite ends of the tunnel. As the workmen came close together they could hear the other team, and they dug, according to the inscription, "pickaxe against pickaxe" until the water flowed from the spring to the reservoir.

Hezekiah's tunnel was a remarkable engineering project for the times. The height of the tunnel varies greatly [note added by Jim D., 5-15 feet] but averages 6 feet, and the water is most often less than knee-deep. Even today visitors to Jerusalem can wade through the s-shaped tunnel in the cool waters of the Gihon spring. Hezekiah was successful in securing the city's water supply. But the prophet (Isaiah 22:9-11) warns Judah's leaders that dependence on defense projects would not be sufficient to secure the city itself." [1]

King Hezekiah loved God with all of his heart and is remembered as a "good king" of Judah even today. But he made a huge mistake that many leaders still make today. The tunnel, the broad wall and other man-made fortifications and plans were not sufficient to protect Jerusalem from the wrath of their enemies. Why not? Because these were man's solutions, not God's solutions!

God had previously shown His **AWESOME** (capitalized because only God should be referred to as Awesome!) power earlier in Hezekiah 's reign when, through the power of God, Sennacherib's army of 185,000 was wiped out by God in a single evening without the help of even one member of Hezekiah's forces (see 2 Kings 19:35-37 and the second article in this series, Revival Before the Fall). Nevertheless, Isaiah warned the leaders of Judah (perhaps including Hezekiah) that dependence on man-made defenses for Jerusalem instead of seeking their Maker, Almighty God, would lead to defeat and captivity for Jerusalem and Judah (Isaiah 22:11)! Isaiah's specific message from God to Judah is recorded in Isaiah 22:14: *"Then it was revealed in my hearing by the Lord of hosts, "Surely for this iniquity **there will be no atonement for you**, Even to your death, says the Lord God of hosts."*

Reflection:

Hezekiah's Tunnel. The tunnel height varied from 5 feet at the entrance to 16 feet inside the gates of Jerusalem with an average width of 23-26 inches. Water still flows through the tunnel today and is an often visited site by tourists to the Holy Land.

Was there really anything wrong with Hezekiah's plan to construct a water tunnel to protect Jerusalem in the event of an attack? Logically speaking, the answer is **"No!"** The tunnel and the protection of the water supply for Jerusalem was a wise move on Hezekiah's part. After all, without access to a continuous water supply, Jerusalem would ultimately fall to an enemy attack.

So what was wrong with constructing the tunnel? Could it be that **their faith was placed in solutions that they fashioned themselves** rather than in God? God's solutions don't always follow man's logic patterns. Was it logical that

God, without any help from man, brought about the defeat and death of Sennacherib's entire 185,000 man army the night before they were poised to attack and destroy Jerusalem? **Most certainly not!** It was Almighty God that brought that about totally on His own.

The Bible clearly teaches that God provides for and protects His own. **God never fails! God's plans are always right! God's plans always work!** He sent Jesus to save us from our sins! He gave the Holy Spirit to believers to abide in us and act on our behalf in accordance with God's will. ALL that He requires of us once we accept Jesus is that we live in accordance with His revealed Word as found in the Bible. Living a life depending on self and without accepting Jesus as Lord and Savior is opposed to God's will. So the lesson of this article is that we should live our life in accordance with the right plan, God's Plan! **Successful Execution of the Wrong Plan**, our plan, is the wrong plan! Allowing God to control the execution of the right plan, His plan, is the only plan!

Our twenty-first century U.S. political leaders are much like the political leaders of Israel and Judah prior to and during their fall to the Assyrians and Babylonians. Instead of putting their faith in God, the Creator and Ruler of ALL, they make their own plans, put their faith in other gods, and assume that they can legislate solutions ... solutions through unholy political alliances, spending enormous funds on wasteful projects, providing endless foreign aid, constructing offensive and defensive weapons, developing advanced technological surveillance solutions such as drones, satellites, computers, etc., etc., etc. All of man's plans and solutions combined will never equal **just one** of the Creator's solutions. No one, no thing, nothing at all can match His plans. He is the one and only Almighty God!

Isaiah's warning to Judah and Jerusalem in Isaiah 22:14 rings in my ears! *"Surely for this iniquity there will be no atonement for you ..."* Are our leaders listening? I don't think so!

You might want to review another of my articles on a related subject, If You Want to Hear God Laugh, Tell Him You Have a Plan.

Where to Read More:

- Scriptures About Hezekiah - 2 Kings 18 – 20; 2 Chronicles 29 – 32; Isaiah 36 – 39
- Biography of King Hezekiah
- Hezekiah's Tunnel - Ferrell Jenkins

04 - Intentional Deceit – The Lies and Intimidation of Sennacherib

Background:

Sennacherib – King of Assyria – Sennacherib during his Babylonian war.
Relief from his palace in Nineveh (Public Domain)

The year is 701 BC. The holy city of Jerusalem is in a terribly fragile condition. While a generally peaceful situation exists within the walls of Jerusalem, all of Israel and the vast majority of Judah lie under the control of Assyria. The welcome reforms put into place by King Hezekiah of Judah are well beyond being threatened ... they are on the verge of vanishing at the hands of the Assyrians.

Hezekiah has purged the city and the Temple of idolatry and regular Temple worship has been reinstated. The "high places" of perverted worship have been destroyed and the cherished Passover celebration has been restored. Nevertheless, Assyrian King Sennacherib's army is camped outside the walls of the holy city of Jerusalem, where Hezekiah is in residence, and poised to attack.

Before the battle, Sennacherib sends three of his military leaders to the walls of the city of Jerusalem with a message for King Hezekiah and the inhabitants of Jerusalem. Sennacherib's message provides an opportunity for modern day Christians to gain insight into how God's followers are tempted to abandon God's teachings and to believe in Satan's lies. In addition, there is also occasion to look into how our leaders are following their own chosen course rather than that of Almighty God.

Scripture: (all Scripture ESV unless otherwise noted)

2 Kings 18:13-16, 36-37 – *13 In the fourteenth year of King Hezekiah, Sennacherib king of Assyria came up against all the fortified cities of Judah and took them. 14 And Hezekiah king of Judah sent to the king of Assyria at Lachish, saying, "I have done wrong; withdraw from me. Whatever you impose on me I will bear." And the king of Assyria required of Hezekiah king of Judah three hundred talents of silver and thirty talents of gold. 15 And Hezekiah gave him all the silver that was found in the house of the LORD and in the treasuries of the king's house. 16 At that time Hezekiah stripped the gold from the doors of the temple of the LORD and from the doorposts that Hezekiah king of Judah had overlaid and gave it to the king of Assyria. ...*

36 But the people were silent and answered him not a word, for the king's (Hezekiah) command was, "Do not answer him." 37 Then Eliakim the son of Hilkiah, who was over the household, and Shebna the secretary, and Joah the son of Asaph, the recorder, came to Hezekiah with their clothes torn and told him the words of the Rabshakeh.

Discussion:

Sennacherib, King of Assyria, has led his powerful army on a successful rampage through Judah intimidating, sacking one Judean city after another and carrying off captives as slaves. His ultimate goal ... attack and defeat the royal and holy city of Jerusalem where King Hezekiah of Judah resides.

According to 2 Kings 18:15-16, in an attempt to ward off the impending attack, Hezekiah paid a tribute of *"all the silver that was found in the house of the LORD and in the treasuries of the king's house. At that time Hezekiah stripped the gold from the doors of the temple of the LORD and from the doorposts that Hezekiah king of Judah had overlaid and gave it to the king of Assyria."*

Below, according to the archeological artifact known as the Taylor prism, are King Sennacherib's own words describing how he viewed the situation with Jerusalem and King Hezekiah:

Taylor Prism

Translated Inscription on Taylor Prism

Because Hezekiah, king of Judah, would not submit to my yoke, I came up against him, and by force of arms and by the might of my power I took 46 of his strong fenced cities; and of the smaller towns which were scattered about, I took and plundered a countless number. From these places I took and carried off 200,156 persons, old and young, male and female, together with horses and mules, asses and camels, oxen and sheep, a countless multitude; and Hezekiah himself I shut up in Jerusalem, his capital city, like a bird in a cage, building towers round the city to hem him in, and raising banks of earth against the gates, so as to prevent escape... Then upon Hezekiah there fell the fear of the power of my arms, and he sent out to me the chiefs and the elders of Jerusalem with 30 talents of gold and 300 talents of silver, and diverse treasures, a rich and immense booty... All these things were brought to me at Nineveh, the seat of my government.

The tribute paid by Hezekiah did nothing to stop the advance of Sennacherib's forces. Instead, Sennacherib positioned his army *"at the aqueduct of the Upper Pool, on the road to the Washerman's Field"* (2 Kings 18:17, NIV) on the outskirts and outside the wall of Jerusalem. The three key messengers (supreme commander, chief officer and field commander) of Sennacherib's army called for King Hezekiah to come out and hear Sennacherib's message. Instead, *"... there came out to them Eliakim the son of Hilkiah, who was over the household, and Shebnah the secretary, and Joah the son of Asaph, the recorder"* (2 Kings 18:18).

Faithfully delivering Sennacherib's message of intimidation and lies, the three Assyrian army leaders boasted about the ease with which they had accomplished their previous victories; the failure of Judah's supposed ally, Egypt, to come to their aid and provide chariots and horses to help protect Judah; and, the superiority of Assyria's god over Judah's God and all other gods.

In addition the messengers tried to turn Hezekiah's own forces against him through lies and deceit by calling *"... out in a loud voice in the language of Judah (Hebrew): 'Hear the word of the great king, the king of Assyria! ... Do not let Hezekiah deceive you, for he will not be able to deliver you out of my hand. Do not let Hezekiah make you trust in the LORD by saying, The LORD will surely deliver us, and this city will not be given into the hand of the king of Assyria.' 31 Do not listen to Hezekiah, for thus says the king of Assyria: 'Make your peace with me and come out to me. Then each one of you will eat of his own vine, and each one of his own fig tree, and each one of you will drink the water of his own cistern, 32 until I come and take you away to a land like your own land, a land of grain and wine, a land of bread and vineyards, a land of olive trees and honey, that you may live, and not die. And do not listen to Hezekiah when he misleads you by saying, "The LORD will deliver us"* (2 Kings 18:28-32).

Reflection:

Drawing some parallels from this article to our modern times, here are some questions that Satan or your enemies might ask as he/they try to foist their wicked ways upon you through intimidation and lies.

- **In Whom/What do you trust?** – Satan often uses such a question to see if your beliefs are on solid ground or can be easily shaken. Believers are often too eager to share dialogue with their enemies thinking that they might be able to persuade them to see things their way.

Recall how Satan posed a simple question in the Garden of Eden to Eve that ultimately led to Adam and Eve's downfall into sin. In Genesis 3:1 Satan approached Eve by herself and asked " ... *"Did God actually say, 'You shall not eat of any tree in the garden'?"* That kind of questioning is designed to bring about doubt in your mind that can lead to doubt in your heart and a lack of trust. Sennacherib used a similar strategy with Hezekiah and the people of Jerusalem by tempting to them to question the adequacy of God (and Hezekiah's defenses) to protect them. Bottom line, place your trust in the King of Kings and Lord of Lords! He will never fail you ... no matter the circumstances!

- **Does the one you trust have your best interest at heart?** – This was certainly the tactic Satan used on Eve in the Garden of Eden. Satan went straight after God launching a direct character assault by saying "... *You will not surely die. [5] For God knows that when you eat of it* (the Tree of Life) *your eyes will be opened, and you will be like God, knowing good and evil* "(Genesis 3:4b-5). Satan was implying that God did not have Eve's best interest at heart. Instead, He was protecting His territory by trickery and deception. Sennacherib also attacked the character of Hezekiah and his God. As recorded in his own words "... by the might of **my** power I took 46 of his strong fenced cities ... and plundered a countless number." In the mind of Sennacherib this implied that his god was far stronger than Judah's God ... and if Judah's God had Jerusalem's best interest at heart, then why would He allow the sacking of most of Judah and the advance of Sennacherib's army all the way to the walls of Jerusalem? Christian, don't allow yourself to be so easily tricked into questioning if following God is worth the price when so many around you seem to be prospering by following Satan's sinful ways. God loves you and wants the very best for you.

- **How secure are you with your King?** – Sennacherib preyed upon the people of Jerusalem's insecurity in both their king and their God. Christian, when you allow yourself to engage in such a conversation, you are more easily led into a state of insecurity. This allows Satan to prey upon that insecurity and place thoughts and questions into your mind such as "Why should I resist? I know it is wrong, but others are doing it and seem to be prospering." Instead, stand firm on your convictions and *"Trust in the LORD with all your heart, and do not lean on your own understanding. In all your ways acknowledge Him, and He will make straight your paths."* (Proverbs 3:5-6). God has never made even one promise that He has not, nor will not, be kept.

- **Is the god you are worshiping really God?** – Finally Satan's (and Sennacherib's) assault reaches a climax by shouting that your God is not real! He is dead! He is simply a figment of your imagination! A trickster! A deceiver! A liar! Not really THE KING at all! Under such an attack it is so easy to fall prey to sin. Everywhere we look ... TV, movies, at work, at school, in our literature, in our government, on the internet ... we see sin at work in our society. Where people were once proud to be Christians, we now see those same people cowered down, afraid to let it be known that they are followers of Almighty God, excluded from conversations, ridiculed and persecuted for their beliefs, forced to accept unGodly acts such as abortion and same-sex marriage, etc., etc.

Christian, you can trust in Almighty God to protect you from Satan's **intentional deceit through his lies and intimidation.** I have read the back of the Holy Book and God is the eternal victor! Satan is a trickster! ... a deceiver! ... a liar!

Anyone not found written in the book of life Let them be cast into the lake of fire.
~Revelation 20:15

John records in Revelation 20:10, "*And the devil that deceived them was cast into the lake of fire and brimstone, where the beast and the false prophet are, and shall be tormented day and night for ever and ever.*" Followers of Satan will suffer the same consequence for an unimaginable eternity. On the other hand, followers of God will spend an unimaginable eternity in Heaven at the feet of Jesus.

Unfortunately the leadership of our modern day world as a whole has fallen prey to practicing the same kinds of lies and deceit used by Satan. Politicians regularly and knowingly lie/deceive constituents to conceal their true agenda. This is almost a universal practice and is an absolute abomination. How can citizens place their trust in a government that lies to them? ... and lies without any concern or consequence when caught in those lies. If you cannot trust your government to tell you the truth about small things, then how can you trust them to tell you the truth about anything? And how can you trust them to provide the protection in the times of crisis. Take a current world situation as an example. Russia places troops next to Crimea, foments unrest using paid thugs, all the time says they have no intent of invading ... and then takes over Crimea anyway. Now they are doing the same thing to the remainder of Ukraine ... massing troops on the border of Ukraine, constantly telling the world that they have no intent to intervene militarily, fomenting unrest using paid thugs, and all the time lying about their real intent.

As Americans, let me pose the same questions mentioned above on an individual level to you about our American government:

- In Whom/What do you trust?
- Does the one you trust have your best interest at heart?
- How secure are you with your King?
- Is the god you are worshiping really God?

Repeating the closing from the third article in this series ...

"Isaiah's warning to Judah and Jerusalem in Isaiah 22:14 rings in my ears! "Surely for this iniquity there will be no atonement for you ..." **Are our leaders listening? I don't think so!"**

Where to Read More:

- Scriptures About Hezekiah - 2 Kings 18 – 20; 2 Chronicles 29 – 32; Isaiah 36 – 39
- Biography of King Hezekiah

05 - The Folly of Not Trusting God – Isaiah Pronounces Judgment

Background:

Leadership is essential for the prosperity of a nation. If the leadership is corrupt, then the nation will most likely be corrupt. Corruption breeds more corruption. If the leadership is Godly, then the nation has a better chance to be Godly. Godliness breeds more Godliness.

Recalling the history described earlier in previous articles in this series, Israel and Judah had entered a dark time in their history as once again the leadership and the people wavered from their trust in God in favor of compromises and alliances. The northern kingdom of Israel was under constant attack from Assyria for decades. With the sacking of Samaria (the capital city of Israel) in 722 BC, all ten tribes of the northern kingdom fell to the Neo-Assyrian Empire. The long and bloody warfare leading to their fall was conducted in multiple waves by the Assyrian monarchs Tiglath-Pileser III (747-727 BC), Shalmaneser V (727-722 BC), and Sargon II (722-705 BC). The Bible records that Israel's defeat was because "... *the children of **Israel had sinned** against the Lord their God ...* (see 2 Kings 17:5-12)."

But for Judah, Hezekiah (715 BC – 686 BC - a good king and son of Ahaz) provided hope that the southern kingdom of Judah would escape the onslaught of the Assyrians. Hezekiah brought about excellent religious reforms to Judah, turning away from the sinful leadership of his father Ahaz. Hezekiah led Judah to return to the worship of Yahweh and relied upon God for direction and protection ... well, not entirely! You see, in preparation for the ultimate siege by Assyria, Hezekiah formed a military alliance with Egypt, an unGodly nation. Egypt would provide horses and horsemen in the event that Judah was attacked by Assyria. This alliance was of men and not ordained by God. Assyria overran almost all of Judah leaving only Jerusalem standing. The Egyptian alliance proved to be useless to Hezekiah and Judah confirming **The Folly of Not Trusting God**. Nevertheless, with the repentance of the nation, God would protect Jerusalem from the ravages of Sennacherib's army of 185,000 soldiers.

Scripture: (all Scripture ESV unless otherwise noted)

Isaiah 31:1-5 — *Woe to those who go down to Egypt for help and rely on horses, who trust in chariots because they are many and in horsemen because they are very strong, but do not look to the Holy One of Israel or consult the LORD! ² And yet he is wise and brings disaster; he does not call back his words, but will arise against the house of the evildoers and against the helpers of those who work iniquity. ³ The **Egyptians are man, and not God**, and their horses are flesh, and not Spirit. When the LORD stretches out His hand, the helper will stumble, and he who is helped will fall, and they will all perish together. ⁴ For thus the LORD said to me, "As a lion or a young lion growls over his prey, and when a band of shepherds is called out against him he is not terrified by their shouting or daunted at their noise, so the LORD of hosts will come down to fight on Mount Zion and on its hill. ⁵ Like birds hovering, so the LORD of hosts will protect Jerusalem; he will protect and deliver it; he will spare and rescue it."*

⁶ Turn to Him from whom people have deeply revolted, O children of Israel. ⁷ For in that day everyone shall cast away his idols of silver and his idols of gold, which your hands have sinfully made for you. ⁸ "And the Assyrian shall fall by a *sword, **not of man**; and a sword, **not of man**, shall devour him; and he shall flee from the sword, and his young men shall be put to forced labor. ⁹ His rock shall pass away in terror, and his officers desert the standard in panic," declares the LORD, whose fire is in Zion, and whose furnace is in Jerusalem.*

Discussion:

Isaiah's words of wisdom found in chapter 31:1-5 clearly relate **The Folly of Not Trusting God**. Egypt was well-known for its advanced cavalry. They had strong horses, strong chariots, strong horsemen. So it seemed natural to form an alliance with Egypt for added protection against the Assyrians. But the alliance between Judah and Egypt was an unholy alliance and would prove faulty and unproductive. A lesson here: **God opposes such relationships for His children with workers of iniquity**. Matthew Henry's commentary relates "Sinners may be convicted of (their) folly by plain and self-evident truths, which they cannot deny, but will not believe. There is no escaping the judgments of God; and evil pursues sinners." Israel was wasting its time with Egypt.

Lion Protecting Kill

On the other hand Isaiah confirms that God will provide all that is required to defend Jerusalem without the help of others. God and His people do not need alliances ... especially with the unGodly. God will serve as the Lion "growling over his prey" (Isaiah 31:4) with fearless might and will not be distracted from His mission by "shouting and noise." Although Judah has not fully trusted God and done evil through the alliance with Egypt, God Himself will, of his own grace, provide the help that Judah needs.

Mother Hen Protecting Her Chicks.

Isaiah continues to describe the certainty of God's protection for His people by providing the example of how a mother hen (bird) protects her offspring under her wings (Isaiah 31:5) in the times of danger. The protection will be provided with compassion and affection. The Lord God Almighty will defend Jerusalem without the help of Egypt. He will make sure that Jerusalem's safety is preserved. It is unnecessary to have a fail-safe defense dependent upon man. God will handle it on His own.

The words of Jesus on this subject are recorded in Matthew 23:37: *"O Jerusalem, Jerusalem, the city that kills the prophets and stones those who are sent to it! How often would I have gathered your children together as a hen gathers her brood under her wings, and you were not willing."*

God promises through Isaiah that He will deliver Jerusalem if they return to Him. *"Turn to Him from whom people have deeply revolted, O children of Israel. (Isaiah 31:6)"* It will be necessary for them to repent and to return to God from their backsliding. Such repentance is always necessary.

Consider these additional scriptures:

- Ezekiel 16:62-63 – *"I will establish my covenant with you, and you shall know that I am the LORD, 63 that you may remember and be confounded, and never open your mouth again because of your shame, when I atone for you for all that you have done, declares the Lord GOD.*

- Hosea 6:1 – "Come, let us return to the LORD; for he has torn us, that he may heal us; he has struck us down, and he will bind us up."

Judah must give up their idols of silver and gold and turn back to God. Healing will result. Misery will be replaced by contentment and confidence in The Lord's protection. Isaiah pronounces judgment on the Assyrians. They will fall not by the act of man, but by the act of God through His angel. As a result of God's actions, Sennacherib, with the loss of his entire army, will flee home alone and Jerusalem will be protected until another day.

Reflection:

God has blessed our nation since its founding in 1776. We have not been without our major flaws ... slavery included. We have fought a war of independence, a shameful civil war, two World Wars and a number of other lesser wars. The Civil War Trust says "roughly 1,264,000 American soldiers have died in the nation's wars ... 620,000 in the Civil War and 644,000 in all other conflicts. It was only as recently as the Vietnam War that the amount of American deaths in foreign wars eclipsed the number who died in the Civil War." In comparison, worldwide deaths from World War II alone amounted to 60 million or 2.5% of the world population at that time.

The current state of affairs in America is quite similar to that of Israel and Judah in the time of Hezekiah and Sennacherib. There are enemies both within and without. There are fears for our safety from just about every corner of the world. We face real threats from terrorism in our cities, our seaports, at diplomatic outposts around the world, on the high seas and even within the relative safety of our own borders.

At the same time, our volunteer military forces are taxed to the limit and have recently had to cut their defense budget in such a significant manner that we can only be involved in one war theater at a time going forward because of financial constraints.

Our leadership has been dealing with the most significant financial crisis since the Great Depression as the country becomes more indebted to unfriendly and foreign entities such as China. The Federal Reserve is artificially holding down interest rates to never before experienced levels supposedly to stimulate the economy, but the action is only marginally working. The unemployment and underemployment rates are at all-time highs since the Great Depression.

Competition to hire recent college graduates is almost non-existent as many students cannot find employment in their specialty field, are taking jobs well below their qualification levels, and many have returned home to live with their parents until the situation improves.

Same-sex marriage, a ridiculous thought less than ten years ago, has been embraced and supported by our highest ranking leadership and is now legal in 17 states. Abortion ... the outright murder of unborn babies ... has been legalized since 1973 and the lives of almost 56 million God-created souls have been brutally and senselessly sacrificed on the fires of Tophet (see my article On Child Sacrifice).

Five sovereign nations (United States, Russian Federation, United Kingdom, France, China) now have the capability to destroy entire populations with their nuclear arsenals. Pakistan, India and the rogue nation of North Korea have also detonated nuclear weapons. Israel is thought to have the ability to deliver a nuclear strike. Iran, one of the staunch enemies of Israel dedicated to the destruction of Israel is actively developing a nuclear weapons capability right in the face of world powers. One mistake or intentional act of terrorism could lead to a worldwide nuclear disaster.

While all of this turmoil is going on the three branches of our government (Executive, Legislative, Judicial) are in complete gridlock ... totally unable to legislate, totally unable to agree on just about anything ... continually blaming each other for everything that is wrong ... agreeing on nothing productive.

Is there a way out of this seemingly hopeless mess? The answer is **YES!** God recorded His solution in 2 Chronicles 7:14 – *"if my people who are called by my name humble themselves, and pray and seek my face and turn from their wicked ways, then I will hear from heaven and will forgive their sin and heal their land."*

So the answer is for us as individual Christians, and our nation as a whole, to get down on our knees, admit we are sinners in need of a Savior, ask God to forgive us of our sins, and allow Him to gain control of our lives, the lives of our leadership, and our future as a nation. God has promised that He will hear and heal! God never makes a promise that He does not keep.

We can start this process in our homes and our churches. We need a revival like we have never seen in modern times. An awakening of the church liken to that found in Acts chapter two. An awakening of the fire of God's holy love. An awakening of devotion to God in our hearts and families. An awakening of a nation that serves God not just in private but in public. An awakening that allows us to know with absolute assurance that we may depend upon God to protect us … no matter the circumstances … just as he did Hezekiah and Jerusalem when they were faithful to Him!

Where to Read More:

- Scriptures About Hezekiah - 2 Kings 18 – 20; 2 Chronicles 29 – 32; Isaiah 36 – 39
- Biography of King Hezekiah

06 - God Listens and Restores – Hezekiah's Illness and Recovery

Background:

Does God change His mind? That is a question that has perplexed man for thousands of years. Malachi 3:6 declares, *"For I the LORD do not change; therefore you, O children of Jacob, are not consumed."* James 1:17 tells us, *"Every good gift and every perfect gift is from above, coming down from the Father of lights with whom there is no variation or shadow due to change."* The meaning of Numbers 23:19 is quite clear: *"God is not man, that he should lie, or a son of man, that he should change his mind. Has he said, and will he not do it? Or has he spoken, and will he not fulfill it?"*

No, God does not change His mind. God is unchanging and unchangeable. God is *sovereign* and *immutable*. *Sovereign* in that God, as the ruler of the Universe, has the right to do whatever he wants and is in absolute control over everything that happens (see Psalm 115:3; Daniel 4:35; Romans 9:20). *Immutable* in the sense that "God is unchanging in his character, will, and covenant promises." God, as the creator and the ruler of the Universe and beyond, has the right to do whatever he wants.

So, hearken back to our chronicle on the times of Hezekiah and let's tie this together. It is 701 BC. We have reached the point in this series of articles where Hezekiah is facing a personal health crisis. A crisis that usually leads to a speedy death.

Scripture: (all ESV unless otherwise noted)

2 Kings 20:1-11 (also found in Isaiah 38) - *In those days Hezekiah became sick and was at the point of death. And Isaiah the prophet the son of Amoz came to him and said to him, "Thus says the LORD, 'Set your house in order, for you shall die; you shall not recover.'" ² Then Hezekiah turned his face to the wall and prayed to the LORD, saying, ³ "Now, O LORD, please remember how I have walked before you in faithfulness and with a whole heart, and have done what is good in your sight." And Hezekiah wept bitterly. ⁴ And before Isaiah had gone out of the middle court, the word of the LORD came to him: ⁵ "Turn back, and say to Hezekiah the leader of my people, Thus says the LORD, the God of David your father: I have heard your prayer; I have seen your tears. Behold, I will heal you. On the third day you shall go up to the house of the LORD, ⁶ and I will add fifteen years to your life. I will deliver you and this city out of the hand of the king of Assyria, and I will defend this city* **for my own sake and for my servant David's sake.** *⁷ And Isaiah said, "Bring a cake of figs. And let them take and lay it on the boil, that he may recover."*

⁸ And Hezekiah said to Isaiah, "What shall be the sign that the LORD will heal me, and that I shall go up to the house of the LORD on the third day?" ⁹ And Isaiah said, "This shall be the sign to you from the LORD, that the LORD will do the thing that he has promised: shall the shadow go forward ten steps, or go back ten steps?" ¹⁰ And Hezekiah answered, "It is an easy thing for the shadow to lengthen ten steps. Rather let the shadow go back ten steps." ¹¹ And Isaiah the prophet called to the LORD, and he brought the shadow back ten steps, by which it had gone down on the steps of Ahaz.

Discussion:

For continuity and additional clarity in the scripture discussion let's explore some of the pertinent history related to this incident. The Thomas Nelson Chronological Study Bible (p. 652) has an excellent summary perfect for our purpose:

"Sargon of Assyria decisively put down the Ashdod rebellion in 712 B.C., and as Isaiah had expected, Egypt did not keep its promises of aid. King Hezekiah must not have been too involved in the rebellion, however, because Judah was not punished as Ashdod was. Nevertheless, a few years later he began to consider rebellion again. He even received overtures of friendship from Merodach-Baladan, who had been driven from Babylon by Sargon around 710 BC but had managed to regain control of planning another rebellion against Assyria.

The biblical history of the next few years appears not only in 2 Kings 18:13-20:21, but also in Isaiah 36-39. The order of events in the biblical text is not strictly chronological. Hezekiah's illness (Isaiah 38) and the visit by ambassadors from the Babylonian ruler Merodach-Baladan (Isaiah 39) are described at the end of this section but must have come before Sennacherib withdrew from Jerusalem (Isaiah 37:37; see 2 Kings 20:6)

The name "Berodach-Baladan" in 2 Kings 20:12 appears to be a corrupted spelling of Merodach-Baladan. He was the Babylonian ruler at two separate times (721-710 and 703-702 BC), and specialized in forming alliances to support his fight against Assyrian control. He may still have been known by the title "king of Babylon at the time of Hezekiah's sickness although he might then have been in exile. Hezekiah died in 686 BC; his illness 15 years earlier would have been approximately 701 BC (2 Kings 20:6)."

King Hezekiah in a 17th-century painting by unknown artist in the choir of
Sankta Maria kyrka in Åhus, Sweden.

Hezekiah had contracted a terrible illness as recognized by the
presence of a significant boil ... an illness that would be certain
to lead to a speedy death. 2 Kings 20:1-11 is our focal
scripture reference. As he had often done before, Isaiah went
to advise Hezekiah in his time of distress. Isaiah gave
Hezekiah the news that he would **most surely die** from his
illness. Hearing this Hezekiah immediately turned his face
toward the wall, and while bitterly weeping, petitioned God for
deliverance from the ravages of the fatal disease. Hezekiah
pleaded with God that he had walked before Him in truth, with
a loyal heart, and had done what was good (and right) in God's
sight. **God listened** to Hezekiah's prayer **and restored** him to
health. Even before Isaiah could leave Hezekiah's presence,
the Word of the Lord came to Isaiah confirming Hezekiah's
healing. Hezekiah would have fifteen more years of life to

build upon his Godly reforms and could continue to protect Jerusalem against the assault of the Assyrian army. Hezekiah asked for a sign from God that He would keep His word. God provided confirmation through a physical sign of His promise to Hezekiah... a sign only God could give.... by miraculously moving the shadow on the sundial backward by ten degrees just as Hezekiah had asked.

A natural question arises here. Did God change His mind regarding Hezekiah's future and instead heal him of his fatal illness? If you followed what was included in the background above, then you know the answer. NO, GOD DID NOT CHANGE HIS MIND! I conclude that God was simply waiting for Hezekiah's repentance and admission that he was totally dependent upon God Himself to provide a solution. God was waiting for Hezekiah to reach the point where he knew that only God was able to deliver him from this terrible scourge.

Reflection:

In times of great distress, men's prayers are often filled with petitions to God to change the course of what seems to be inevitable. Some point to specific scriptures, often taken out of context, to cite instances where God changed His mind. But this is simply not true. God does not change His mind. He could, but He won't. Repeating Numbers 23:19 which is quite clear: "*God is not man, that he should lie, or a son of man, that he should change his mind.* **Has he said, and will he not do it? Or has he spoken, and will he not fulfill it?**"

I am reminded of a hauntingly similar event in an earlier slice of time for Israel and Judah.

Rehoboam – Fragment of the wall painting in the Great Council Chamber of Basel Town Hall. – Hans Holbein the Younger (1498–1543)

Rehoboam, son of Solomon and grandson of David, had come to the throne of (2 Chronicles 11-12) the United Kingdom of the twelve tribes. In approximately 931 BC the ten northern tribes revolted against the leadership and harsh tax treatment of Rehoboam and separated themselves into the Northern Kingdom of Israel led by

Jeroboam sets up two golden calves, from the Bible Historiale. Den Haag, MMW, 10 B 23 165r
Date 1372

Jereboam (931-910 BC). Rehoboam then governed only the Southern Kingdom of Judah. Both Rehoboam and Jereboam were considered as "bad" kings forsaking the Law of the Lord.

In the fifth year of Rehoboam's reign, God's prophet, Shemaiah, told Rehoboam and all of the princes of Judah gathered in Jerusalem that Judah would be overrun and defeated by Shishak of Egypt (1 Kings 14:25; 2 Chronicles 12:1-12). Why? **Because Rehoboam and Judah had forsaken God.** Shishak had provided Jereboam sanctuary earlier and was considered an ally of Israel. According to the Bible, Shishak took all of the fortified cities of Judah and carried off many of the treasures of the temple and the royal palace in Jerusalem, including the "shields of gold" that Solomon had made. Jerusalem was spared to some degree because " ... *the princes of Israel and the king humbled themselves; and they said, The Lord is righteous. And when the Lord saw that they humbled themselves ... the Lord said ... because they have humbled themselves ... I will not destroy them, but I will grant them some deliverance. Nevertheless, they shall be his servants; that they may know my service ... (2* Chronicles 12:5-8 KJV, some minor paraphrase on my part)."

As was the case with Hezekiah, did God change His mind about the fate of Reheboam and Jerusalem? The answer is obvious! God does not change His mind. No, He waits for us to recognize our sin, repent of that sin and then and only then carries out His perfect will in the lives of men.

Much like Judah, is there hope for America? Are we in a temporary respite from the wrath of God? Can we survive our sickness as a nation unto death like Hezekiah? Is there any hope that we will not go the way of Israel and Judah and ultimately fall to our enemies under the weight of our own sin? Current circumstances in America don't seem to point to a way of escape from the consequences of our individual and collective sin because we, and our leaders, continue to ignore the will of God for our nation.

However, I do believe the scripture teaches there is always hope ... hope that is sure, hope that is lasting, hope that is without fail, hope that is found only in Almighty God. Hope that is found through repentance. Hope that is found because of God's love and His perfect will.

So why is it so hard for man to find real and worthy direction and answers to life's problems? Could it be that our sin simply blinds us from seeing the truth? After all, God recorded ALL of His solutions in His Word, the Bible. God's answers to our ALL of our problems are enumerated within its pages. There are ample examples in the Bible of how righteousness breeds success for nations and unrighteousness breeds doom. Could it be that we are too modern and too sophisticated to believe that an ancient God and His time-proven life principles are still at work? Could it be that we have become so dependent upon our selves and our governments that we no longer see the need for God? Could it be that even if we believe in an Almighty God that we don't trust Him enough to allow Him to provide for ALL of our needs?

Has America reached a point in our history where we refuse to recognize that we must individually and collectively as a nation **seek first** the kingdom of God? (*But seek first the kingdom of God and his righteousness, and all these things will be added*

to you Matthew 6:33). Is it more important to live in an era of political correctness, inclusiveness and sensitivity, all the while shunning the appearance of anything Christian?

To me the course of action for America is obvious. Our sinfulness does indeed blind us from seeing the truth. It separates us from God. It provides false hope. It leads us to destructive paths of unrighteousness. It causes despair ... lack of trust in one another ... disgust with our leaders. Our sin is a death spiral leading to self-destruction!

In summary, there are some scriptural principles involved here.

- First of all, there must be recognition that **God is God and man is not God**.
- God is the author of ALL that is good and right.
- Satan and man are the authors of ALL things corrupt and sinful.
- There are no flaws in God's plans.
- Man-made solutions to our problems, no matter what they might be, are ALLWAYS inferior to those of God.
- None of our other gods including items such as fame, self-dependence, self-righteousness, military forces, government, wealth (money, gold, silver jewels, etc.), prosperity, freedom, legislation, rules, alliances, compromises, contracts, commitments, covenants, treaties, promises, bond or judge can ever begin to match the solutions of the one and only supreme Jehovah God.

American leaders have abandoned God. How soon will God abandon us? Are we ready to admit that we are a sinful nation? Are we ready to humble ourselves? Are we ready to repent as a nation? Are we ready for God to heal our nation? Until we do as King Hezekiah did, then wallowing in our national sinful condition will continue unabated.   May God help us!

Where to Read More:

- Scriptures About Hezekiah - 2 Kings 18 – 20; 2 Chronicles 29 – 32; Isaiah 36 – 39
- Biography of King Hezekiah

07 - Lest Any Man Should Boast – Sennacherib Blasphemes Jehovah

Background:

I have done my share of boasting and bragging over my life. Reflecting back, most of my boasting was harmful, though I did not necessarily understand the harm that I was doing at the time. Boasting is often s a ruse that allows one to elevate himself above his peers, or to turn peers into pawns. Sometimes boasting is designed just to tear others down ... to implant fear in others ... to elevate self over others, undeservedly.

Boasters often claim credit for a result as a work of their own, refusing to give credit to the one who actually was responsible for the accomplishment. The most insidious example of this is when one expects to earn a permanent place in heaven through their own initiative by steadfastly adhering to a set of rules and/or by doing good works. The Bible teaches that this is utter foolishness and that man's salvation and home in Heaven can only be obtained through the grace of God because of what HE HAS DONE! Ephesians 2:4-9 puts it this way:

> *4 But God, being rich in mercy, because of the great love with which he loved us, 5 even when we were dead in our trespasses, made us alive together with Christ— by grace you have been saved— 6 and raised us up with Him and seated us with Him in the heavenly places in Christ Jesus, 7 so that in the coming ages he might show the immeasurable riches of his grace in kindness toward us in Christ Jesus. 8 For by grace you have been saved through faith. And this is not your own doing; it is the gift of God, 9 not a result of works, so that no one may boast.*

Let's look closer at boasting/bragging by examining more closely what the Bible says about King Sennacherib of Assyria as he boasted to Hezekiah and Jerusalem against Jehovah God. (For a more detailed review of the situation surrounding this article, you might want to review my article, Intentional Deceit, before proceeding with the rest of this article, though it is not necessary if time does not permit.)

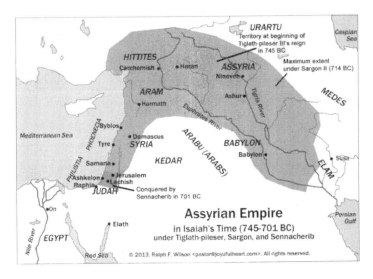

First, some additional background derived from *Thomas Nelson's Chronological Study Bible* (2008, p.673, A Bird in a Cage). In the 8th century BC the Assyrians were the dominant power in the Near East region of the ancient world. The confrontation between King Hezekiah of Judah and King Sennacherib of Assyria is well chronicled in the Bible and also in the annals of Assyrian history. Assyrian historical records claim that at the time of this boastful confrontation, Sennacherib had already destroyed 46 walled cities in Judah and numerous smaller towns. Sennacherib claimed that he had taken 200,150 Judeans captive in the process.

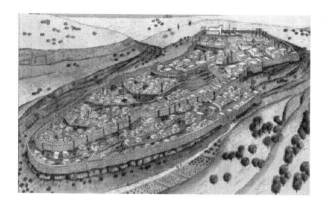

Artist's depiction of Jerusalem at the time of Hezekiah showing the second wall.

This was a severe blow to Judah, bordering on catastrophe. Sennacherib's army next surrounded Jerusalem and seemed fully equipped to finish the absolute conquest of Judah. The Assyrian Chief of Staff Rabshakeh tried to convince Jerusalem's city leaders to approach King Hezekiah to peacefully surrender the city without a fight. Sennacherib's historical writings boasted about Hezekiah: "Himself like a caged bird, I shut up in Jerusalem, his royal city."

Jerusalem was terrified. But God had a plan. Isaiah prophesied that under God the Assyrian army would withdraw and Sennacherib would meet his demise without taking Jerusalem.

Scripture:

2 Chronicles 32:9-23 – *⁹After this, Sennacherib king of Assyria, who was besieging Lachish with all his forces, sent his servants to Jerusalem to Hezekiah king of Judah and to all the people of Judah who were in Jerusalem, saying, ¹⁰ "Thus says Sennacherib king of Assyria, 'On what are you trusting, that you endure the siege in Jerusalem? ¹¹ Is not Hezekiah*

misleading you, that he may give you over to die by famine and by thirst, when he tells you, "The LORD our God will deliver us from the hand of the king of Assyria"? ^{12} Has not this same Hezekiah taken away his high places and his altars and commanded Judah and Jerusalem, "Before one altar you shall worship, and on it you shall burn your sacrifices"? ^{13} Do you not know what I and my fathers have done to all the peoples of other lands? Were the gods of the nations of those lands at all able to deliver their lands out of my hand? ^{14} Who among all the gods of those nations that my fathers devoted to destruction was able to deliver his people from my hand, that your God should be able to deliver you from my hand? ^{15} Now, therefore, do not let Hezekiah deceive you or mislead you in this fashion, and do not believe him, for no god of any nation or kingdom has been able to deliver his people from my hand or from the hand of my fathers. How much less will your God deliver you out of my hand!'"

^{16} And his servants said still more against the LORD God and against his servant Hezekiah. ^{17} And he wrote letters to cast contempt on the LORD, the God of Israel, and to speak against him, saying, "Like the gods of the nations of the lands who have not delivered their people from my hands, so the God of Hezekiah will not deliver his people from my hand." ^{18} And they shouted it with a loud voice in the language of Judah to the people of Jerusalem who were on the wall, to frighten and terrify them, in order that they might take the city. ^{19} And they spoke of the God of Jerusalem as they spoke of the gods of the peoples of the earth, which are the work of men's hands.

^{20} Then Hezekiah the king and Isaiah the prophet, the son of Amoz, prayed because of this and cried to heaven. ^{21} And the LORD sent an angel, who cut off ALL the mighty warriors and commanders and officers in the camp of the king of Assyria. So *he returned with shame of face to his own land. And when he came into the house of his god, some of his own sons struck him down there with the sword.* ²² *So the LORD saved Hezekiah and the inhabitants of Jerusalem from the hand of Sennacherib king of Assyria and from the hand of all his enemies, and he provided for them on every side.* ²³ *And many brought gifts to the LORD to Jerusalem and precious things to Hezekiah king of Judah, so that he was exalted in the sight of all nations from that time onward.*

Discussion:

II Chronicles 32:9 begins with the words "After **this** ... " What is the "**this**?" Sennacherib had already sacked most of Judah carrying off over 200 thousand captives. In an attempt to placate Sennacherib and save Judah and Jerusalem from destruction, Hezekiah paid a significant tribute to the Assyrian King, greatly decreasing Judah's remaining national treasury. The tribute was gladly accepted but did not stop Sennacherib from continuing his assault on Judah.

Relief showing Judean captives being led away into slavery by the Assyrians after the siege of Lachish in 701 B.C. Source: www.en.wikipedia.org/wiki/File:Lachishsieg

Almost immediately Sennacherib's army laid siege to the city of Lachish located twenty-five miles southwest of Jerusalem, completely sacking the Judean city. Immediately Sennacherib sent his representatives to Jerusalem to deliver his boasting message demanding the surrender of Jerusalem without a battle. According to The Wycliffe Bible Commentary (1962, The Moody Bible Institute of Chicago, pp. 415-416) Sennacherib hoped to capitalize on any unpopularity of the Godly reforms (32:1) imposed by Hezekiah such as the removal of the "high places" of perverted worship (32:12). In addition Sennacherib's spokesmen committed blasphemy against Jehovah God boasting that Judah's God was no more able to protect them than any of the other gods of the cities that Assyria had already conquered (32:14). The verbal assault was extended to a written assault (32:17).

*"Then Hezekiah the king and Isaiah the prophet, the son of Amoz, **prayed** because of this and cried to heaven (32:20)."*
God answered their prayer by sending an angel to "*...cut off all the mighty warriors and commanders and officers in the camp of the king of Assyria (32:21).*" Sennacherib's army surrounding Jerusalem at that point consisted of 185,000 men ... quite a sizable force. The entire force was killed in one night through a supernatural event totally the work of Jehovah God (32:21). This event, like the crossing on dry ground of the Red Sea during the Exodus from Egypt, is one of the most significant examples of how God intervenes to save his chosen people when they have repented and are on the right path. Sennacherib, spared when the angel delivered death to his entire army, returned to Assyria "*with shame of face*" to the "*house of his god* (where) *some of his own sons struck him down there with the sword (32:21).*"

So the LORD saved Hezekiah and the inhabitants of Jerusalem from the hand of Sennacherib king of Assyria and from the hand of ALL his enemies, and he provided for them on every side (32:22). The treasury in Jerusalem, depleted by the tribute paid by Hezekiah to Sennacherib, was wondrously restored through the generous gifts of "many" (32:23).

Reflection:

There are at least three moral lessons we can learn from this article:

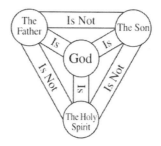

The Holy Trinity – The Triune God

- First, there is a **supreme price to pay if you blaspheme** against any form of the Triune God (Father, Son, Holy Spirit. Boasting and bragging about how great you and your god(s) are will not go unnoticed by God! Recognize that God, and only God, is supreme. Man's boasting about himself and his accomplishments are in vain.
- Second, **God will protect and deliver those who are faithful** to Him, no matter the seeming odds stacked against them.
- Third, **Boasting should never be about ourselves and our accomplishments**. Boasting should always be about God. Consider Jeremiah 9:23-24 – *Thus says the Lord: "Let not the wise man **boast** in his wisdom, let not the mighty man **boast** in his might, let not the rich*

*man **boast** in his riches, 24 but let him who **boasts boast** in this, that he understands and knows me, that I am the Lord who practices steadfast love, justice, and righteousness in the earth. For in these things I delight, declares the Lord."*

Sennacherib boasted about himself and his gods. He and his army paid the ultimate price through the actions of Almighty God. Will America pay the ultimate price because of our boasting about ourselves? Or will be do as Hezekiah and Isaiah did? Will we give up our self-centered independence from God? Will we admit both our individual and collective sinfulness as a people and as a nation? Will we turn from / repent from our wicked ways? Will we seek God through prayer with a broken heart asking for forgiveness that only He can provide? Will we seek His help to bring about Godly reforms in our homes, our churches, our public places and especially in our government? Will we no longer boast and brag about ourselves but only about God? Are we ready to stem the tide in America or stand aside and witness anew "**The Fall of a Godly Nation**?"

I pray that we are ready to turn away from ourselves and to God as our refuge in the times of such great trouble.

For Additional Study:

See Appendix A for Scriptures on Boasting – Jude 1:16; Proverbs 27:1; Proverbs 25:14; Judges 9:38; 1 Samuel 2:1-3; Psalms 10:3; Amos 4:5; Matthew 6:2; Proverbs 27:2; 1 Corinthians 3:21; James 3:14; James 4:16; Jeremiah 9:23-24; Psalms 75:5.

Click here to look up the scriptures and display in a browser on website **Bible Gateway.** Click here for a printable pdf file format of these scriptures.

08 - Parading Your Own Glory – The Consequences of Hezekiah's Pride

Background:

King Hezekiah of Judah had trusted God to heal him of his deathly illness (see <u>God Listens and Restores – Hezekiah's Illness and Recovery</u>). In 702/701 BC Assyrian King Sennacherib's mighty army had been totally destroyed at the gates of Jerusalem by the hand of Almighty God. Sennacherib returned to Nineveh totally defeated. Some twenty years later in 681 BC, as the dejected Sennacherib worshiped his pagan god Nisroch, two of his sons assassinated him with a sword and fled to Ararat (now consisting of parts of Iran, Iraq and southern Russia), Assyria's enemy to the north. Another of Sennacherib's sons, Esarhaddon, took over the throne of Assyria. II Kings 19:35-37 records the events:

"*35 And that night the angel of the LORD went out and struck down 185,000 in the camp of the Assyrians. And when people arose early in the morning, behold, these were all dead bodies. 36 Then Sennacherib king of Assyria departed and went home and lived at Nineveh. 37 And as he was worshiping in the house of Nisroch his god, Adrammelech and Sharezer, his sons, struck him down with the sword and escaped into the land of Ararat. And Esarhaddon his son reigned in his place.*"

For the time being, Jerusalem and the Temple had again been spared by God's own hand and remained safely under the leadership of King Hezekiah. But would that safety last?

Scripture: (all ESV unless otherwise noted)

Isaiah 39:1-8 – *At that time Merodach-baladan the son of Baladan, king of Babylon, sent envoys with letters and a* *present to Hezekiah, for he heard that he had been sick and had recovered. ² And Hezekiah welcomed them gladly. **And he showed them his treasure house, the silver, the gold, the spices, the precious oil, his whole armory, all that was found in his storehouses. There was nothing in his house or in all his realm that Hezekiah did not show them.** ³ Then Isaiah the prophet came to King Hezekiah, and said to him, "What did these men say? And from where did they come to you?" Hezekiah said, "They have come to me from a far country, from Babylon." ⁴ He said, "What have they seen in your house?" Hezekiah answered, **"They have seen all that is in my house. There is nothing in my storehouses that I did not show them."***

*⁵ Then Isaiah said to Hezekiah, "Hear the word of the LORD of hosts: ⁶ Behold, **the days are coming, when all that is in your house, and that which your fathers have stored up till this day, shall be carried to Babylon. Nothing shall be left, says the LORD.** ⁷ And some of your own sons, who will come from you, whom you will father, shall be taken away, and they shall be eunuchs in the palace of the king of Babylon." ⁸ Then Hezekiah said to Isaiah, "The word of the LORD that you have spoken is good." For he thought, "There will be peace and security in my days."*

Discussion:

Hezekiah's dependence upon God for delivery from the Assyrians was short-lived. Instead of giving God ALL of the glory for the defeat of Sennacherib's army, Hezekiah fell prey to his own pride.

Hearing of Hezekiah's severe illness and miraculous recovery, King Merodach-baladan of Babylon, the son of Baladan, sent envoys with gifts and letters to Jerusalem. King Hezekiah welcomed them with open arms ... but he made a key mistake ... a mistake that would ultimately lead to the fulfillment of Isaiah's prophecy that Judah and ALL of its treasures would be carried away to Babylon (Isaiah 39:5-7). Hezekiah's **prayers had been replaced by his pride** as he **paraded his own glory**, not the glory of God (39:1-2). Hezekiah simply could not tell the envoys that ALL that had happened was the direct result of Almighty God's providence. Instead, Hezekiah took credit for the vast treasures that had been accumulated by Judah solely as a result of God's actions.

2 Chronicles 32:31 gives more insight into the surfacing of Hezekiah's pride: "*31 And so in the matter of the envoys of the princes of Babylon, who had been sent to him to inquire about the sign that had been done in the land, God **left him to himself, in order to test him and to know all that was in his heart**.*" Hezekiah was tested and his pride won the battle within his heart.

Reflection:

Why is it that we are so anxious to point out what we view as major sins such as adultery, homosexuality or racism and at the same time ignore those areas that we often attempt to hide from others. The sin of pride is one such sin. Pride can ruin our testimony and hinder our relationship with God.

God's word has so much to say about our pride (see Bible Verses on Pride or Appendix B. Pride is a deceptive device of Satan. Proverbs 6:17 lists "haughty eyes" as the first among seven things that are an abomination to God. In the words of Jesus Himself recorded in Luke 18:14, "*I tell you, this man went down to his house justified, rather than the other. **For everyone who exalts himself will be humbled**, but the one who humbles himself will be exalted.*" Our pride reveals a truth about us. In a sense we are saying that we don't need God. We can do things without Him. We are sufficient on our own.

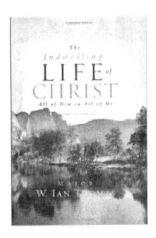

But God created us in such a way that His Spirit is to reside within us and act out through us. That is the way He made us. Every true Christian has the Holy Spirit of God dwelling within their heart as soon as they accept Jesus as their Savior. Acting on our own instead of allowing the Holy Spirit to act on our behalf is not part of God's plan for man. I am thrilled with the way that Major Ian Thomas explains this concept in his book "The Indwelling Life of Christ – All of Him in All of Me."

"God has created us to be functional only by virtue of His presence, exercising His divine sovereignty within our humanity so that out of our love for Him, we live in utter dependence upon Him. Moreover, the only evidence any of us can give of such dependence on Him is our unquestioning obedience to Him.

That is the threefold moral relationship — love for Him, dependence upon Him, and obedience to Him — that allows God to be God in action within a human being."

There is simply no room for pride if we allow the Holy Spirit to act from within us. God has His perfect plan all laid out for us. Attempting to live our life on our own leads to a path of self-destruction. No one knows this better than God for He has seen how pride has destroyed the lives of His creations from the beginning.

Pride is revealed in the way that we interact with others. It reveals our attitude and tells us that we should be the center of attention ... look at me and what I have done! Pride keeps us from accepting just criticism of ourselves and causes us to disdain the successes of others.

In his book, _Mere Christianity_, C.S. Lewis said, "A proud man is always looking down on things and people; and, of course, as long as you are looking down, you cannot see something that is above you." Looking up to the Master and listening to Him with the eyes of your heart will undoubtedly turn you away from your prideful attitude. Let's face it, if Jesus was willing to wash the Disciples feet (John 13:1-17), is there anything that we can rightfully refuse to do as His servants?

Sennacherib's boasting and pride led to the destruction of his army and ultimately to his death by the hands of his own sons.

When Hezekiah faced certain death he repented, prayed and trusted God for healing from his deadly sickness and God healed him, extending his life for 15 more years. But Hezekiah, servant that he was of God, made a significant mistake by letting his pride get the best of him. He let his pride take over and by **parading his own glory** revealed ALL of Judah's treasures to the Babylonian envoys paving the way for Judah to ultimately be carried off into captivity by Babylon.

Is our nation really that much different from Israel and Judah of old? The answer to most of our problems was presented to us by Almighty God long ago through the life, death and resurrection of His Son Jesus Christ. In his life on earth as a man Jesus was a true servant … always without pride … never boastful. He commanded the power of the universe but never used that power for Himself. Instead, He humbled Himself for us and went to the cross of Calvary to pay the price for ALL of man's sins … including the sin of pride.

Are you **Parading Your Own Glory**? Or are you putting your pride aside in favor of allowing God's plan to work in your life? **Parading your pride does not bring glory to God.** Instead it is directly out of the will of God … and there are consequences that will be suffered.

Where to Read More:

- Bible Verses on Pride – see Appendix B
- Scriptures About Hezekiah - 2 Kings 18 – 20; 2 Chronicles 29 – 32; Isaiah 36 – 39
- Biography of King Hezekiah

09 – Passing the Mantle – The Failure of a Godly Father

Background:

Looking back at my last article, <u>Parading Your Own Glory – The Consequences of Hezekiah's Pride</u>, we learned that King Hezekiah remained on the throne of Judah only through the providence and protection of Almighty God. Suffering from a disease certain to result in his death, Hezekiah pleaded for healing from God and was miraculously healed extending his life for fifteen more years. Additionally, God, and God alone, destroyed Assyrian King Sennacherib's massive army of 185,000 warriors poised at the gates of Jerusalem in only one night causing Sennacherib to flee back to his home in Assyria where he would eventually be assassinated by two of his own sons.

When Babylon's King Merodach-Baladan heard about Hezekiah's miraculous healing and the way that God delivered Jerusalem from certain slaughter by Sennacherib's army, he sent envoys to Hezekiah with messages and gifts of congratulations. Instead of praising God for "**His**" deliverance Hezekiah bragged to the envoys about "**his**" accomplishments rather than those of Jehovah God. Hezekiah pridefully (and shamefully) exposed the entire contents of the treasury of Jerusalem and the Temple to the envoys. This vain and quite naive act by Hezekiah and other future serious transgressions by Judah's leadership would eventually result in their final downfall and captivity in 587 BC to the Babylonian Empire.

This article picks up with King Hezekiah still on the throne of Judah in the year 702 BC. It will discuss Isaiah's warning from God to Hezekiah, explore the transition of the throne from Hezekiah to his son Manasseh, discuss some of the highlights of Manasseh's reign and conclude with a life lesson especially for fathers.

Scripture: (all ESV unless otherwise noted)

2 Kings 21:1-18 – *Manasseh was twelve years old when he began to reign, and he reigned fifty-five years in Jerusalem. His mother's name was Hephzibah.* ^{2} *And **he did what was evil in the sight of the** Lord, according to the despicable practices of the nations whom the Lord drove out before the people of Israel.* ^{3} *For **he rebuilt the high places** that Hezekiah his father had destroyed, and **he erected altars for Baal** and made an Asherah, as Ahab king of Israel had done, and worshiped all the host of heaven and served them.* ^{4} *And he built altars in the house of the Lord, of which the Lord had said, "In Jerusalem will I put my name."* ^{5} *And he built altars for all the host of heaven in the two courts of the house of the Lord.* ^{6} *And he burned his son as an offering$^{[a]}$ and used fortune-telling and omens and dealt with mediums and with necromancers. He did much evil in the sight of the Lord, provoking him to anger.* ^{7} *And the carved image of Asherah that he had made he set in the house of which the Lord said to David and to Solomon his son, "In this house, and in Jerusalem, which I have chosen out of all the tribes of Israel, I will put my name forever.* ^{8} *And I will not cause the feet of Israel to wander anymore out of the land that I gave to their fathers, if only they will be careful to do according to all that I have commanded them, and according to all the Law that my servant Moses commanded them."* ^{9} ***But they did not listen, and Manasseh led them astray to do more evil than the nations had done whom the Lord destroyed before the people of Israel.***

^{10} *And the Lord said by his servants the prophets,* ^{11} *"**Because Manasseh king of Judah has committed these abominations** and has done things more evil than all that the Amorites did,* who were before him, and has made Judah also to sin with his idols, *12 therefore thus says the Lord, the God of Israel:* **Behold, I am bringing upon Jerusalem and Judah such disaster**[b] *that the ears of everyone who hears of it will tingle. 13 And I will stretch over Jerusalem the measuring line of Samaria, and the plumb line of the house of Ahab, and **I will wipe Jerusalem as one wipes a dish, wiping it and turning it upside down.** 14 And I will forsake the remnant of my heritage and give them into the hand of their enemies, and they shall become a prey and a spoil to all their enemies, 15 **because they have done what is evil in my sight** and have provoked me to anger, since the day their fathers came out of Egypt, even to this day."*

*16 Moreover, **Manasseh shed very much innocent blood**, till he had filled Jerusalem from one end to another, besides the sin that **he made Judah to sin so that they did what was evil in the sight of the Lord.***

17 Now the rest of the acts of Manasseh and all that he did, and the sin that he committed, are they not written in the Book of the Chronicles of the Kings of Judah? 18 And Manasseh slept with his fathers and was buried in the garden of his house, in the garden of Uzza, and Amon his son reigned in his place.

See also Isaiah 39, II Chronicles 32:33-33:20, Jeremiah 15:4 … not included here for brevity, but pertinent to the article.

Discussion:

The Bible records little detail on the final fifteen years of Hezekiah's reign. Other sources, such as those from the Jewish organization Chabad.org, indicate that Hezekiah's final years were "peaceful and happy." Chabad goes on to say that God's blessings brought wealth in gold, silver and spices into

Jerusalem along with the return of some of the Jews previously exiled. Chabad also states that the Temple was the only center of worship and the practice of idolatry was minimized seemingly concluding that all was well in Judah. But realistically, all was not well in Judah!

Isaiah 39 records a prophetic encounter that took place between Isaiah and Hezekiah. In this encounter God specifically told Hezekiah through Isaiah that *"the days are coming, when **ALL** that is in your house, and that which your fathers have stored up till this day, **shall be carried to Babylon**. Nothing shall be left, says the Lord. ⁷And some of your own sons, who will come from you, whom you will father, shall be taken away, and they shall be eunuchs in the palace of the king of Babylon."* Hezekiah's pitiful response to Isaiah response reveals the depth of his selfishness at this time: ⁸ ... *"The word of the Lord that you have spoken is good."* For he thought, *"**There will be peace and security in my days**."* In other words, this won't be my problem ... why should I prepare anyone to deal with it ... it is not going to happen on my watch ... it will happen after I am gone through my descendants ... so why should I worry about it? And he didn't!

Further confirming Hezekiah's selfishness II Chronicles 32:25 records: *"But Hezekiah did not make return according to the benefit done to him, for his heart was proud. Therefore wrath came upon him and Judah and Jerusalem."*

Description English: Manasses was a king of the Kingdom of Judah. He was the only son and successor of Hezekiah. Date in 1553 Source "Promptuarii Iconum Insigniorum " Author Published by Guillaume Rouille(1518?-1589)

Hezekiah had one son, Manasseh (meaning "to forget"), born in 709 BC. Manasseh, an ancestor of Christ (see Matthew 1:10) through David's son Solomon, was an impressionable boy seven years of age when God delivered Judah from Sennacherib's army in 702 BC. Five years later in 697 BC Manasseh became co-regent of Judah at the age of twelve. He served at his father's side for ten years as an *apprentice* until Hezekiah's death in 687 BC. He then became sole regent and would reign until 643 BC for a total of 55 years (2 Kings 21:1; 2 Chronicles 33:1). This was the longest reign of all of the Kings of Judah.

History records that while Hezekiah was a "good" king, Manasseh was a "bad" king. So, what happened that led Manasseh to abandon the path of his father and be remembered until this day as a "bad" king?

When Hezekiah died in 687 BC, Manasseh, now 22 years of age, did an about-face by reversing his father's religious and political reforms. Manasseh dishonored God as many other kings had done (including his grandfather Ahaz) by forming unholy political alliances with surrounding pagan nations. He re-established the worship of their powerless pagan gods ... even placing their idols in the Temple!

Manasseh's Idolatry

Following the despicable practice of the pagans (see my article On Child Sacrifice), II Chronicles 33:6 records that Manasseh *"burned his sons as an offering in the Valley of the Son of Hinnom, and used fortune-telling and omens and sorcery, and dealt with mediums and with necromancers."*

Manasseh's fall into paganism and the adoption of the religious practices of his enemies ultimately led to his capture by the Assyrians and his forceful captivity in Babylon (II Chronicles 33:10-11). In captivity and under great distress Manasseh finally repented as he *"humbled himself greatly before the God of his fathers"* (II Chronicles 33:12). God heard his sincere penitent prayer and returned Manasseh to Jerusalem where he went about reversing his evil practices. **But it was too late for Jerusalem and Judah** ... as God told Hezekiah and now Manasseh ... Judah will fall into complete destruction at the hands of the Babylonians. And they did!

Reflection:

It is a bit of speculation on my part, but I have concluded, based on my study of the Scriptures, that Hezekiah failed Manasseh in his fatherly responsibilities. The lack of humility, obedience to God, and everyday selfish example set by Hezekiah before Manasseh during the final years of his reign were key factors leading to Manasseh's failure as Judah's leader. Instead of nurturing his son in the ways of the Lord in his younger years and preparing Manasseh for his sole reign as Judah's king, Hezekiah simply stayed true to his own selfish ways. Under such circumstances there is little doubt in my mind that Manasseh concluded that his father was not interested in his future or the future of Judah and that his best course of action was to make alliances with his enemies. Clearly this was the wrong decision.

With Manasseh's death in 643 BC six more kings would lead Judah as they continued on the path to their final destruction as a nation in 587 BC ending the line of Davidic kings. The links below will lead you to articles on each king.

- Amon – son of Manasseh 643/642 – 641/640 BC
- Josiah – son of Amon – 641/640 – 610/609 BC
- Jehoahaz – son of Josiah – 3 months in 609 BC
- Jehoiakim – son of Josiah – 609 – 598 BC
- Jeconiah/Jehoiachin – son of Jehoiakim – 3 months 598 – 597 BC
- Zedekiah – son of Josiah – appointed by Nebuchadnezzar II of Babylon – 597 – 587 BC

A once powerful and Godly nation was destined to fall because of their own sin and the sin of their leaders. Are we really that different from Israel and Judah? I don't think so!

In days gone by the United States of America had a strong set of Judeo-Christian values. We point back with pride to our Christian heritage. Today that heritage is under attack from all sides. Christians are suffering mounting persecution in the open and free practice of their faith. Paganism is on the rise as rebellion against Almighty God continues to spread. Our nation has legalized the slaughter of millions upon millions of babies through abortion ... much like the pagan practices adopted during Manasseh's reign. We are creeping ... perhaps even running ... further and further from the worship of the one and only true God as we satisfy our fleshly desires. What we need as a nation is old-fashioned personal and national repentance. The examples provided by Israel and Judah outlined in this series of articles are ample warning that we, too, are headed for destruction as a people and a nation if we do not repent and turn to God.

II Chronicles 7:14 provides the only real answer for us ... *"if my people who are called by my name humble themselves, and pray and seek my face and turn from their wicked ways, then I will hear from heaven and will forgive their sin and heal their land."* The key to healing our nation must start with the Christian. Christians must first humble themselves, pray, seek God's face and turn away from their wickedness. As the momentum grows our nation can be healed and spared by God.

Life Lesson:

Proverbs 22:6 (ESV) tells us, "Train up a child in the way he should go;
even when he is old he will not depart from it."

The Bible teaches that it is the responsibility of parents to provide spiritual training for their children. It is the parents' job to raise their children in a manner such that they will conduct their lives in accordance with God's plan, His will, and His purpose for their lives. As a result of such Godly training children develop a faith in God that will see them through the most difficult of times and prepare them to face the constant onslaught of Satan throughout their lives. Such lives honor God and strengthen not only the children's faith, but the faith of communities, and ultimately nations.

Children emulate the behavior of their parents. When a child observes his or her parents living according to Godly principles and not just talking about them, they will follow the parents' lead. Likewise, when a child observes the hypocritical, selfish or lackadaisical behavior of the parent ... where words do not match deeds ... then confusion reigns in the mind of the child and destroys any positive effect of parental teaching.

God has assigned a major priority to parents to personally provide spiritual training to their children during their formative years. Proverbs 22:6 (ESV) tells us, *"Train up a child in the way he should go; even when he is old he will not depart from it."* Sadly, far too many parents neglect this portion of their child-rearing responsibilities, leaving most spiritual instruction to someone else.

Children need daily spiritual instruction from their parents ... *"You shall teach them diligently to your children, and shall talk of them when you sit in your house, and when you walk by the way, and when you lie down, and when you rise"* (Deuteronomy 6:7). In his sermon "Training Our Children," Dr. Charles Stanley relates that parents are required to prepare their " ... sons and daughters to walk according to God's plan, will, and purpose for their lives" ... and "are to instill in them an unshakable faith that will protect them from the assault of the Devil." You can view an excerpt from Dr. Stanley's message here.

The personal investment that parents make in the spiritual training of their children will directly affect the rest of the children's lives. Spiritual training provides a strong foundation for building love and respect for God, purity, character, obedience, righteousness, reverence, integrity, morality, trustworthiness, loyalty, bravery, benevolence and many other desirable qualities.

Where to Read More:

- Scriptures About Hezekiah – 2 Kings 18 – 20; 2 Chronicles 29 – 32; Isaiah 36 – 39
- Scriptures About Manasseh – 2 Kings 21:1-18, Isaiah 39, 2 Chronicles 32:33-33:20, Jeremiah 15:4, Matthew 1:10
- Biography of King Hezekiah
- Biography of King Manasseh
- Training Our Children – Excerpt from Dr. Charles Stanley's Message

10 – Conclusion: Is It Too Late For America?

Background:

When I started assembling the material that eventually morphed into a book, I had in mind writing just a couple of articles recalling a specific time in the history of ancient Israel and Judah that parallel the times we live in today in the early twenty-first century. It seemed to me that an important message for our generation was clear: Israel and Judah were on a sure path to self-destruction, and today most, if not all, of the nations of the world are on a similar path. Sadly, this includes the United States of America. Why? Because of our individual and collective sinfulness and disobedience to the commands of the one and only Almighty Jehovah God!

Realizing that I would not be able to cover the breadth of the material God was placing in my heart in such a condensed format, I began the journey knowing that it would likely take several months of prayer, study, research and multiple articles to faithfully convey the full content and message. What I did not know at the time was that it would take almost a year to complete the task! I struggled with medical issues and some of the content but tried to remain non-political, though at times that was very difficult.

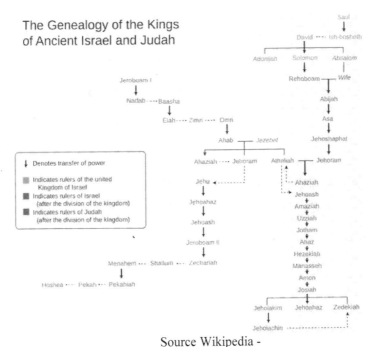

The Genealogy of the Kings
of Ancient Israel and Judah

Source Wikipedia -
http://en.wikipedia.org/wiki/Davidic_line#mediaviewer/File:Genea
logy_of_the_kings_of_Israel_and_Judah.svg

The Bible teaches that the fall of Israel and Judah as once
Godly nations resulted from **their own continued sinfulness
and disobedience to God's commands** ... not from the
strength and power of their enemies. Quite to the contrary,
after giving Israel and Judah countless "second" chances to
repent of their sins and return to Him, God finally had enough
of their rebellion and **He allowed** their enemies to overwhelm
them and take them into captivity thus completing **The Fall of
a Godly Nation** and ending the rule of the <u>Davidic Kings</u>. As
you can see in the figure depicting the "Genealogy of the Kings
of Ancient Israel and Judah," Hezekiah and Manasseh were
just two of the kings in the lineage ... the former remembered
as a "good" king and the latter as a "bad" king. But the

sinfulness of both leaders and those before and after them contributed to Israel and Judah's demise.

So many of today's religious leaders have passionately preached that America has turned her face away from God. Our nation, our leaders and even many of those who profess to be Christians, as a matter of choice, do not obey God's commandments or live by biblical principles. Is it any wonder that our collective morality as a nation is at an all time low? Regardless of what has led us to our current pitiful position, Christian's should care enough about America to cry out to God on her behalf.

Is it too late for America to be turned away from our path of self-destruction? As a Christian and a patriotic American I believe that the answer is **No**! God is a God of hope! God is a God of promises! His promises are recorded in His Holy Word and He will keep them! God is a God of righteousness and He requires His children to be obedient to His commands!

God will not continue to ignore our unrighteous sinfulness and Godlessness. There are consequences to our individual and collective sin! So, how do we address our downhill slide and reverse **The Fall of a Godly Nation**?

Scripture: (all ESV unless otherwise noted)

2 Timothy 3:1-5 - *But understand this, that in the last days there will come times of difficulty. ² For people will be lovers of self, lovers of money, proud, arrogant, abusive, disobedient to their parents, ungrateful, unholy, ³ heartless, unappeasable, slanderous, without self-control, brutal, not loving good, ⁴ treacherous, reckless, swollen with conceit, lovers of pleasure rather than lovers of God, ⁵ having the appearance of godliness, but denying its power. Avoid such people.*

2 Chronicles 7:14 - *If my people who are called by my name humble themselves, and **pray and seek my face** and turn from their wicked ways, then I will hear from heaven and will **forgive their sin** and **heal their land**.*

Matthew 6:33 - *But **seek ye first** the kingdom of God, and his righteousness; and all these things shall be added unto you.*

Psalm 51:10 - *Create in me a clean heart, O God, and renew a right spirit within me.*

Psalm 85:6 - *Will you not revive us again, that your people may rejoice in you?*

Discussion:

In chapter three of Paul's second letter to Timothy, we find a description of what Paul describes as the "*last days*" and the difficulty that will occur during those days. Consider carefully Paul's description of man's behavior: "*[2] For people will be lovers of self, lovers of money, proud, arrogant, abusive, disobedient to their parents, ungrateful, unholy, [3] heartless, unappeasable, slanderous, without self-control, brutal, not loving good, [4] treacherous, reckless, swollen with conceit, lovers of pleasure rather than lovers of God, [5] having the appearance of godliness, but denying its power.*" The evidence of our sinfulness and disobedience to God that I observe all around us today certainly argues that we are in those last days.

Of this scripture Matthew Henry says there will be ...

"persecution from without ... on account of corruptions within. Men love to gratify their own lusts, more than to please God and do their duty. When every man is eager for what he can get, and anxious to keep what he has, this makes men dangerous to one another. When men do not fear God, they will not regard man. When children are disobedient to their parents, that makes the times perilous. Men are unholy and without the fear of God, because unthankful for the mercies of God. We abuse God's gifts, if we make them the food and fuel of our lusts."

Just as in the days of Hezekiah and Judah, America needs a revival. That revival must start with God's church. America is in such great need of repentance. The church is where our repentance and revival must start. The familiar verse found in 2 Chronicles 7:14 provides the formula for God's solution: *"If My people who are called by My name* **humble themselves**, *and* **pray and seek My face** *and* **turn from their wicked ways**, *then* **I will hear** *from heaven and will* **forgive their sin** *and* **heal their land**."

Note that God says *"My people."* Christians are God's *"My people."* America will never repent until His people ... those called by His name ... Christians ... the church ... pray and turn from their wicked ways. True and lasting solutions to our problems will not and can not come through man's laws, legislation, alliances, treaties, or military might. They will come from God, and God alone!

In His Sermon on the Mount recorded in Matthew 5-7 Jesus stated: *"But* **seek ye first** *the kingdom of God, and His righteousness; and all these things shall be* **added** *unto you (Matthew 6:33)"* ... **added** by Almighty God ... not by man.

Gerard van Honthorst (1590–1656) - King David Playing The Harp

David prayed a sincere prayer of repentance (Psalm 51:1-12) after Nathan the prophet confronted him regarding his sin with Bathsheba. It would do us well as Christians to pray a similar prayer of repentance.

Psalm 51:1-12

1 Have mercy on me, O God,
according to your steadfast love (loving kindness);
according to your abundant mercy
blot out my transgressions.
2 Wash me thoroughly from my iniquity,
and cleanse me from my sin!

3 For I know my transgressions,
and my sin is ever before me.

⁴ Against you, you only, have I sinned
and done what is evil in your sight,
so that you may be justified in your words
and blameless in your judgment.
⁵ Behold, I was brought forth in iniquity,
and in sin did my mother conceive me.
⁶ Behold, you delight in truth in the inward being,
and you teach me wisdom in the secret heart.

⁷ Purge me with hyssop, and I shall be clean;
wash me, and I shall be whiter than snow.
⁸ Let me hear joy and gladness;
let the bones that you have broken rejoice.
⁹ Hide your face from my sins,
and blot out all my iniquities.
¹⁰ Create in me a clean heart, O God,
and renew a right spirit within me.
¹¹ Cast me not away from your presence,
and take not your Holy Spirit from me.
¹² Restore to me the joy of your salvation,
and uphold me with a willing spirit.

Psalm 85 is one of the twenty-five Psalms attributed to the sons of Korah. This Psalm projects a beautiful picture of the desire for true revival. Verse 6 echoes in my mind as I write this article: ***"Will you not revive us again, that your people may rejoice in you?"***

Psalm 85 - Revive Us Again

¹ Lord, you were favorable to your land;
you restored the fortunes of Jacob.
² You forgave the iniquity of your people;
you covered all their sin. Selah.

³ You withdrew all your wrath;
  you turned from your hot anger.

⁴ Restore us again, O God of our salvation,
  and put away your indignation toward us!
⁵ Will you be angry with us forever?
  Will you prolong your anger to all generations?
⁶ Will you not revive us again,
  that your people may rejoice in you?
⁷ Show us your steadfast love, O Lord,
  and grant us your salvation.

⁸ Let me hear what God the Lord will speak,
  for he will speak peace to his people, to his saints;
  but let them not turn back to folly.
⁹ Surely his salvation is near to those who fear him,
  that glory may dwell in our land.

¹⁰ Steadfast love and faithfulness meet;
  righteousness and peace kiss each other.
¹¹ Faithfulness springs up from the ground,
  and righteousness looks down from the sky.
¹² Yes, the Lord will give what is good,
  and our land will yield its increase.
¹³ Righteousness will go before him
  and make his footsteps a way.

Reflection:

We are indeed a nation in need of prayer, repentance and healing. The unGodly condition of present day America is enough to put us on our knees seeking God's divine intervention. God has warned us and continues to warn us. As a nation our rebellion against Him can not be denied! God has not changed! He is the same yesterday, today and tomorrow. Christian, those who are His children, we must get down on our knees and ask God to send a great awakening to America. The future of our nation ... the future of our children and grandchildren ... depends upon our repentance. God has promised ... yes, **PROMISED** ... and God keeps ALL of His promises ... "*If My people who are called by My name humble themselves, and pray and seek My face and turn from their wicked ways, then I will hear from heaven and will forgive their sin and heal their land* (2 Chronicles 7:14)."

History is our teacher. God has been patient with America ... a once **Godly Nation**. Israel/Judah was also a once **Godly Nation**. Israel/Judah suffered their fall. Will America be next to suffer **The Fall of a Godly Nation**? **Is It Too Late For America?** Only time will tell.

Where to Read More:

- Sons of Korah
- A Nation in Need of Prayer

- <u>Bible Verses On Revival</u>

Appendix A

Bible Verses on Boasting (ESV)
A Supplement for the Article
Lest Any Man Should Boast – Sennacherib Blasphemes Jehovah
by
Jim Davenport
www.jimdavenport.me

Jude 1:16; Proverbs 27:1; Proverbs 25:14; Judges 9:38; 1 Samuel 2:1-3; Psalm 10:3; Amos 4:5; Matthew 6:2; Proverbs 27:2; 1 Corinthians 3:21; James 3:14; James 4:16; Jeremiah 9:23-24; Psalm 75:5

Jude 1:16 - These are grumblers, malcontents, following their own sinful desires; they are loud-mouthed boasters, showing favoritism to gain advantage.

Proverbs 27:1 - Do not boast about tomorrow, for you do not know what a day may bring.

Proverbs 25:14 - Like clouds and wind without rain is a man who boasts of a gift he does not give.

Judges 9:38 - Then Zebul said to him, "Where is your mouth now, you who said, 'Who is Abimelech, that we should serve him?' Are not these the people whom you despised? Go out now and fight with them."

1 Samuel 2:1-3 - And Hannah prayed and said, "My heart exults in the Lord; my horn is exalted in the Lord. My mouth derides my enemies, because I rejoice in your salvation. 2 "There is none holy like the Lord: for there is none besides you; there is no rock like our God. 3 Talk no more so very proudly, let not arrogance come from your mouth; for the Lord is a God of knowledge, and by him actions are weighed.

Psalm 10:3 - For the wicked boasts of the desires of his soul, and the one greedy for gain curses and renounces the Lord.

Amos 4:5 - offer a sacrifice of thanksgiving of that which is leavened, and proclaim freewill offerings, publish them; for so you love to do, O people of Israel!" declares the Lord God.

Matthew 6:2 - Thus, when you give to the needy, sound no trumpet before you, as the hypocrites do in the synagogues and in the streets, that they may be praised by others. Truly, I say to you, they have received their reward.

Proverbs 27:2 - Let another praise you, and not your own mouth; a stranger, and not your own lips.

1 Corinthians 3:21 - So let no one boast in men. For all things are yours,

James 3:14 - But if you have bitter jealousy and selfish ambition in your hearts, do not boast and be false to

James 4:16 - As it is, you boast in your arrogance. All such boasting is evil.

Jeremiah 9:23-24 - Thus says the Lord: "Let not the wise man boast in his wisdom, let not the mighty man boast in his might, let not the rich man boast in his riches, 24 but let him who boasts boast in this, that he understands and knows me, that I am the Lord who practices steadfast love, justice, and righteousness in the earth. For in these things I delight, declares the Lord."

Psalm 75:5 - do not lift up your horn on high, or speak with haughty neck.

Appendix B

Bible Verses on Pride (ESV)
A Supplement for the Article
Parading Your Own Glory - The Consequences of Hezekiah's Pride
by
Jim Davenport
www.jimdavenport.me

James 4:6 - But he gives more grace. Therefore it says, "God opposes the proud, but gives grace to the humble."

Proverbs 16:18-19 - Pride goes before destruction, and a haughty spirit before a fall. It is better to be of a lowly spirit with the poor than to divide the spoil with the proud.

Proverbs 16:5 - Everyone who is arrogant in heart is an abomination to the Lord; be assured, he will not go unpunished.

James 4:7 - Submit yourselves therefore to God. Resist the devil, and he will flee from you.

Proverbs 8:13 - The fear of the Lord is hatred of evil. Pride and arrogance and the way of evil and perverted speech I hate.

Luke 10:19-20 - Behold, I have given you authority to tread on serpents and scorpions, and over all the power of the enemy, and nothing shall hurt you. Nevertheless, do not rejoice in this, that the spirits are subject to you, but rejoice that your names are written in heaven."

1 Timothy 1:10 - The sexually immoral, men who practice homosexuality, enslavers, liars, perjurers, and whatever else is contrary to sound doctrine,

Romans 12:2 - Do not be conformed to this world, but be transformed by the renewal of your mind, that by testing you may discern what is the will of God, what is good and acceptable and perfect.

1Timothy 3:6 - He must not be a recent convert, or he may become puffed up with conceit and fall into the condemnation of the devil.

Romans 8:26-27 - Likewise the Spirit helps us in our weakness. For we do not know what to pray for as we ought, but the Spirit himself intercedes for us with groanings too deep for words. And he who searches hearts knows what is the mind of the Spirit, because the Spirit intercedes for the saints according to the will of God.

1 Corinthians 6:19-20 - Or do you not know that your body is a temple of the Holy Spirit within you, whom you have from God? You are not your own, for you were bought with a price. So glorify God in your body.

1 Corinthians 6:19 - Or do you not know that your body is a temple of the Holy Spirit within you, whom you have from God? You are not your own,

1 Corinthians 3:16 - Do you not know that you are God's temple and that God's Spirit dwells in you?

1 Corinthians 2:13 - And we impart this in words not taught by human wisdom but taught by the Spirit, interpreting spiritual truths to those who are spiritual.

Romans 12:1-2 - I appeal to you therefore, brothers, by the mercies of God, to present your bodies as a living sacrifice, holy and acceptable to God, which is your spiritual worship. Do not be conformed to this world, but be transformed by the renewal of your mind, that by testing you may discern what is the will of God, what is good and acceptable and perfect.

Luke 11:13 - If you then, who are evil, know how to give good gifts to your children, how much more will the heavenly Father give the Holy Spirit to those who ask him!"

Isaiah 1:1-31 - The vision of Isaiah the son of Amoz, which he saw concerning Judah and Jerusalem in the days of Uzziah, Jotham, Ahaz, and Hezekiah, kings of Judah. Hear, O heavens, and give ear, O earth; for the Lord has spoken: "Children have I reared and brought up, but they have rebelled against me. The ox knows its owner, and the donkey its master's crib, but Israel does not know, my people do not understand." Ah, sinful nation, a people laden with iniquity, offspring of evildoers, children who deal corruptly! They have forsaken the Lord, they have despised the Holy One of Israel, they are utterly estranged. Why will you still be struck down? Why will you continue to rebel? The whole head is sick, and the whole heart faint.

Romans 8:14 - For all who are led by the Spirit of God are sons of God.

Romans 1:26-27 - For this reason God gave them up to dishonorable passions. For their women exchanged natural relations for those that are contrary to nature; and the men likewise gave up natural relations with women and were consumed with passion for one another, men committing shameless acts with men and receiving in themselves the due penalty for their error.

Luke 20:36 - For they cannot die anymore, because they are equal to angels and are sons of God, being sons of the resurrection.

Isaiah 28:1 - Ah, the proud crown of the drunkards of Ephraim, and the fading flower of its glorious beauty, which is on the head of the rich valley of those overcome with wine!

Ecclesiastes 12:7 - And the dust returns to the earth as it was, and the spirit returns to God who gave it.

Psalm 59:12 - For the sin of their mouths, the words of their lips, let them be trapped in their pride. For the cursing and lies that they utter,

Galatians 5:1 - For freedom Christ has set us free; stand firm therefore, and do not submit again to a yoke of slavery.

Romans 8:15 - For you did not receive the spirit of slavery to fall back into fear, but you have received the Spirit of adoption as sons, by whom we cry, "Abba! Father!"

John 14:16-17 - And I will ask the Father, and he will give you another Helper, to be with you forever, even the Spirit of truth, whom the world cannot receive, because it neither sees him nor knows him. You know him, for he dwells with you and will be in you.

Appendix C – List of Links

The following table contains a list of the embedded links in this book that are neither visible nor "clickable" in a hard copy book. The embedded links refer to specific URL's that make navigation in an online environment much easier and do not significantly interrupt the flow of the document. The links are listed in the order that they appear in the book.

..... 01

Neo-Assyrian Empire▶
http://en.wikipedia.org/wiki/Neo-Assyrian_Empire

Tiglath-Pileser III▶
http://en.wikipedia.org/wiki/Tiglath-Pileser_III

Shalmaneser V▶
http://en.wikipedia.org/wiki/Shalmaneser_V

Sargon II▶
http://en.wikipedia.org/wiki/Sargon_II

On Child Sacrifice▶
http://jimdavenport.me/2012/07/01/on-child-sacrifice/

Neo-Babylonian Empire▶
http://en.wikipedia.org/wiki/Neo-Babylonian_Empire

….. 02

House of David ▶
http://en.wikipedia.org/wiki/Davidic_line

2 Chronicles 29:1▶
https://www.biblegateway.com/passage/?search=2+Chronicles+29%3A1&version=NKJV

King Jotham▶
http://en.wikipedia.org/wiki/Jotham_of_Judah

King Uzziah▶
http://en.wikipedia.org/wiki/Uzziah

2 Kings 19:35-37▶
https://www.biblegateway.com/passage/?search=2+Kings+19%3A35-37&version=NKJV

King Jotham▶
http://www.vtaide.com/gleanings/Kings-of-Israel/biography_Jotham.html

broad wall▶
http://en.wikipedia.org/wiki/Broad_Wall_%28Jerusalem%29

2 Kings 18 - 20; 2 Chronicles 29 - 32; Isaiah 36 - 39▶
https://www.biblegateway.com/passage/?search=2+Kings+18-20%3B+2+Chronicles+29-32%3B+Isaiah+36-39&version=NKJV

Biography of King Hezekiah▶
http://www.vtaide.com/gleanings/Kings-of-Israel/biography_Hezekiah.html

..... 03

Revival Before the Fall▶
http://jimdavenport.me/2014/01/25/revival-before-the-fall/

House of David▶
http://en.wikipedia.org/wiki/Davidic_line

2 Kings 16▶
https://www.biblegateway.com/passage/?search=2+kings%20
16-16&version=NIV

Isaiah 7-9▶
https://www.biblegateway.com/passage/?search=isaiah%207-
9&version=NIV

2 Chronicles 28▶
https://www.biblegateway.com/passage/?search=2+chronicles
%2028-28&version=NIV

Broad Wall▶
http://en.wikipedia.org/wiki/Broad_Wall_%28Jerusalem%29

his healing▶
http://en.wikipedia.org/wiki/Healing_the_man_blind_from_bi
rth

2 Kings 19:35-37▶
https://www.biblegateway.com/passage/?search=2 I Kings+19
%3A35-37&version=NKJV

Revival Before the Fall▶
http://jimdavenport.me/2014/01/25/revival-before-the-fall/

If You Want to Hear God Laugh, Tell Him You Have a Plan▶
http://jimdavenport.me/2012/12/14/if-you-want-to-hear-god-laugh-tell-him-you-have-a-plan/

2 Kings 18 - 20; 2 Chronicles 29 - 32; Isaiah 36 - 39▶
https://www.biblegateway.com/passage/?search=2+Kings+18-20%3B+2+Chronicles+29-32%3B+Isaiah+36-39&version=NKJV

Biography of King Hezekiah▶
http://www.vtaide.com/gleanings/Kings-of-Israel/biography_Hezekiah.html

Hezekiah's Tunnel ▶
http://biblicalstudies.info/hezekiah/hezekiah.htm

..... 04

Taylor prism▶
http://biblicalstudies.info/hezekiah/hezekiah.htm

2 Kings 18 – 20; 2 Chronicles 29 – 32; Isaiah 36 – 39▶
https://www.biblegateway.com/passage/?search=2+Kings+18-20%3B+2+Chronicles+29-32%3B+Isaiah+36-39&version=NKJV

Biography of King Hezekiah▶
http://www.vtaide.com/gleanings/Kings-of-
Israel/biography_Hezekiah.html

..... 05

Neo-Assyrian Empire▶
http://en.wikipedia.org/wiki/Neo-Assyrian_Empire

Tiglath-Pileser III▶
http://en.wikipedia.org/wiki/Tiglath-Pileser_III

Shalmaneser V▶
http://en.wikipedia.org/wiki/Shalmaneser_V

Sargon II▶
http://en.wikipedia.org/wiki/Sargon_II

relates▶
http://www.christnotes.org/commentary.php?com=mhc&b=23
&c=31

The Civil War Trust▶
http://www.civilwar.org/education/history/faq/

60 million or 2.5%▶
http://en.wikipedia.org/wiki/World_War_II_casualties

On Child Sacrifice▶
http://jimdavenport.me/2012/07/01/on-child-sacrifice/

2 Kings 18 – 20; 2 Chronicles 29 – 32; Isaiah 36 – 39▶

https://www.biblegateway.com/passage/?search=2+Kings+18-20%3B+2+Chronicles+29-32%3B+Isaiah+36-39&version=NKJV

Biography of King Hezekiah▶
http://www.vtaide.com/gleanings/Kings-of-Israel/biography_Hezekiah.html

..... 06

Malachi 3:6▶
https://www.biblegateway.com/passage/?search=malachi+3:6

James 1:17▶
https://www.biblegateway.com/passage/?search=james+1%3A17&version=ESV

Numbers 23:19▶
https://www.biblegateway.com/passage/?search=Numbers+23%3A19&version=ESV

Sovereign▶
http://dictionary.reference.com/browse/sovereign

Psalm 115:3; Daniel 4:35; Romans 9:20►
https://www.biblegateway.com/passage/?search=Psalm+115%3A3%3B+Daniel+4%3A35%3B+Romans+9%3A20&version=ESV

Immutable►
http://en.wikipedia.org/wiki/Immutability_%28theology%29#cite_note-1

Chronological Study Bible►
http://www.thomasnelson.com/the-chronological-study-bible

Ashdod►
http://en.wikipedia.org/wiki/Ashdod

Merodach-Baladan►
http://en.wikipedia.org/wiki/Marduk-apla-iddina_II

Numbers 23:19►
https://www.biblegateway.com/passage/?search=Numbers+23%3A19&version=ESV

Rehoboam►
http://en.wikipedia.org/wiki/Rehoboam

Jereboam►
http://en.wikipedia.org/wiki/Jeroboam

Shemaiah►
http://en.wikipedia.org/wiki/Shemaiah_%28prophet%29

Shishak►
http://en.wikipedia.org/wiki/Shishak

1 Kings 14:25►

http://en.wikipedia.org/wiki/Shishak

2 Chronicles 12:1-12▶
https://www.biblegateway.com/passage/?search=2%20Chronicles%2012:1-12

2 Kings 18 – 20; 2 Chronicles 29 – 32; Isaiah 36 – 39▶
https://www.biblegateway.com/passage/?search=2+Kings+18-20%3B+2+Chronicles+29-32%3B+Isaiah+36-39&version=NKJV

Biography of King Hezekiah▶
http://www.vtaide.com/gleanings/Kings-of-Israel/biography_Hezekiah.html

….. 07

Intentional Deceit▶
http://jimdavenport.me/2014/04/22/intentional-deceit/

Near East▶
http://en.wikipedia.org/wiki/Near_East

Click here to look up the scriptures▶
https://www.biblegateway.com/passage/?search=Jude+1%3A16%3B+Proverbs+27%3A1%3B+Proverbs+25%3A14%3B+Judges+9%3A38%3B+1+Samuel+2%3A1-3%3B+Psalm+10%3A3%3B+Amos+4%3A5%3B+Matthew+6%3A2%3B+Proverbs+27%3A2%3B+1+Corinthians+3%3A21%3B+James+3%3A14%3B+James+4%3A16%3B+Jeremiah+9%3A23-24%3B+Psalm+75%3A5+&version=ESV

Click here for a printable pdf file▶
https://docs.google.com/file/d/0B_sm7pNmpvT5Q0tnbWNtd
WY1azQ/edit?pli=1

….. 08

God Listens and Restores – Hezekiah's Illness and
Recovery▶
http://jimdavenport.me/2014/06/05/god-listens-and-restores-
hezekiahs-illness-and-recovery/

see Bible Verses on Pride▶
https://docs.google.com/file/d/0B_sm7pNmpvT5UUJPdWpn
NGVPSUk/edit?pli=1

The Indwelling Life of Christ – All of Him in All of Me▶
http://www.amazon.com/The-Indwelling-Life-Christ-
All/dp/1590525248/ref=sr_1_1?ie=UTF8&qid=1403888348&
sr=8-1&keywords=the+indwelling+major+ian+thomas

Mere Christianity▶
http://www.amazon.com/Mere-Christianity-C-S-
Lewis/dp/0060652926/ref=sr_1_1?ie=UTF8&qid=140391608
0&sr=8-1&keywords=mere+christianity+cs+lewis

Bible Verses on Pride▶
https://docs.google.com/file/d/0B_sm7pNmpvT5UUJPdWpn
NGVPSUk/edit?pli=1

2 Kings 18 – 20; 2 Chronicles 29 – 32; Isaiah 36 – 39▶

https://www.biblegateway.com/passage/?search=2+Kings+18-20%3B+2+Chronicles+29-32%3B+Isaiah+36-39&version=NKJV

Biography of King Hezekiah▶
http://www.vtaide.com/gleanings/Kings-of-Israel/biography_Hezekiah.html

….. 09

Parading Your Own Glory – The Consequences of Hezekiah's Pride▶
http://jimdavenport.me/2014/07/03/parading-your-own-glory-the-consequences-of-hezekiahs-pride/

Isaiah 39▶
https://www.biblegateway.com/passage/?search=Isaiah+39&version=ESV

II Chronicles 32:33-33:20▶
https://www.biblegateway.com/passage/?search=+II+Chronicles+32%3A33-33%3A20&version=ESV

Jeremiah 15:4▶
https://www.biblegateway.com/passage/?search=Jeremiah+15%3A4&version=ESV

Chabad.org▶
http://www.chabad.org/library/article_cdo/aid/464025/jewish/Hezekiahs-Last-Years-of-Reign.htm

Matthew 1:10▶

https://www.biblegateway.com/passage/?search=Matthew+1%3A10&version=ESV

On Child Sacrifice▶
http://jimdavenport.me/2012/07/01/on-child-sacrifice/

Amon▶
http://en.wikipedia.org/wiki/Amon_of_Judah

Josiah▶
http://en.wikipedia.org/wiki/Josiah

Jehoahaz▶
http://en.wikipedia.org/wiki/Jehoahaz_of_Judah

Jehoiakim▶
http://en.wikipedia.org/wiki/Jehoiakim

Jeconiah/Jehoiachin▶
http://en.wikipedia.org/wiki/Jeconiah

Zedekiah▶
http://en.wikipedia.org/wiki/Zedekiah

Nebuchadnezzar II▶
http://en.wikipedia.org/wiki/Nebuchadnezzar_II

Training Our Children▶
http://www.intouch.org/resources/sermon-outlines/Content.aspx?topic=Training_Our_Children_Sermon_Outline

here▶
https://docs.google.com/file/d/0B_sm7pNmpvT5bUl4Ni10X2RsY0E/edit?pli=1

2 Kings 18 – 20; 2 Chronicles 29 – 32; Isaiah 36 – 39▶
https://docs.google.com/file/d/0B_sm7pNmpvT5bUI4Ni10X2
RsY0E/edit?pli=1

2 Kings 21:1-18▶
https://www.biblegateway.com/passage/?search=2+Kings+21
%3A1-18&version=ESV

Isaiah 39▶
https://www.biblegateway.com/passage/?search=Isaiah+39&v
ersion=ESV

2 Chronicles 32:33-33:20▶
https://www.biblegateway.com/passage/?search=+II+Chronicl
es+32%3A33-33%3A20&version=ESV

Jeremiah 15:4▶
https://www.biblegateway.com/passage/?search=Jeremiah+15
%3A4&version=ESV

Matthew 1:10▶
https://www.biblegateway.com/passage/?search=Matthew+1
%3A10&version=ESV

Biography of King Hezekiah▶
http://www.vtaide.com/gleanings/Kings-of-
Israel/biography_Hezekiah.html

Biography of King Manasseh▶
http://en.wikipedia.org/wiki/Manasseh_of_Judah

Training Our Children▶
https://docs.google.com/file/d/0B_sm7pNmpvT5bUI4Ni10X2
RsY0E/edit?pli=1

..... 10

http://en.wikipedia.org/wiki/Davidic_line#mediaviewer/File:G
enealogy_of_the_kings_of_Israel_and_Judah.svg►
http://en.wikipedia.org/wiki/Davidic_line#mediaviewer/File:G
enealogy_of_the_kings_of_Israel_and_Judah.svg

Davidic Kings►
http://en.wikipedia.org/wiki/Davidic_line

persecution from without►
http://www.christnotes.org/commentary.php?b=55&c=3&com
=mhc

Gerard van Honthorst (1590–1656) - King David Playing The
Harp►
http://commons.wikimedia.org/wiki/File:Gerard_van_Honthors
t_-_King_David_Playing_the_Harp_-_Google_Art_Project.jpg

Psalm 51:1-12►
https://www.biblegateway.com/passage/?search=Psalm%2051
&version=ESV

sons of Korah►
http://www.gotquestions.org/sons-of-Korah.html

Sons of Korah►
http://www.gotquestions.org/sons-of-Korah.html

A Nation in Need of Prayer►

http://www.intouch.org/resources/sermon-outlines/Content.aspx?topic=A_Nation_in_Need_of_Prayer_Sermon_Outline

Bible Verses On Revival▶
http://www.openbible.info/topics/revival

Books by Jim Davenport

Christian Devotions and Quick Studies
Thank You Lord for Saving My Soul
Thanksgiving Day – Religious to Secular
The Fall of a Godly Nation

Preview and Order Books by Jim Davenport
http://jimdavenport.me/jims-books/

Jim's books are available for all of the popular eReaders such as the Kindle, Apple iPad/iBooks, Nook, Sony Reader, Kobo, Palm, Web Browser, RTF (viewable with most word processors), PDF, and most PC based e-reading apps including Stanza, Aldiko, and Adobe Digital Editions, among others.

Not everyone wants to go to the internet to read Christian articles and not everyone has a computer … thus I also have printed books available. You can support Jim's writing ministry by purchasing one of his books at this link:

Preview and Order Books by Jim Davenport
http://jimdavenport.me/jims-books/

For additional information address:

Jim Davenport
InfoSys Solutions Associates, Inc.
6637 Burnt Hickory Drive
Hoschton, GA 30548

jimdavenport.me
jamesldavenport@gmail.com